One in Four Women

understanding men's domestic abuse of women

Sandra Reddish

This is a work of non-fiction. However, the author has changed the names and redacted identifying characteristics of certain people to protect privacy.

DAS

www.domesticabuses.com

Editing: Patricia Higham
Illustrations: Phoebe Wood
Formatting: Creative Cat Apps

ISBN 978-1-7396479-0-2

Contents

Introduction

Domestic abuse spans all ages, sexes, cultures and social classes, it does not discriminate. It also takes many forms – men's abuse of women, women's abuse of men, abuse in same sex relationships, abuse by adult children of their parents, abuse by parents of their adult children, abuse by carers and honour-based abuse. Each form of domestic abuse is based on different beliefs, involves different patterns of behaviour, comes with different risk factors and requires different responses. Honour-based abuse is motivated by desire to maintain family honour, abuse of parents by adult children is generally motivated by plans for financial gain, men's abuse of women is motivated by the desire to gain and maintain power and control. This book deals solely with men's abuse of women where there is or has been an intimate relationship. It addresses the most common features of this type of abuse. 'Men' includes all self-identified men. 'Women' includes all self-identified women.

About Me

I gained in-depth knowledge of men's abuse of women having worked with domestic abuse for over 34 years as both a police officer and as an outreach worker at BWP, an inspiring domestic abuse charity in Nottinghamshire. As a police officer, I dealt with the full range of abuse including domestic homicide. I worked with perpetrators, survivors and their children whilst seeing all facets of abuse often soon after the incident had occurred when those involved were in very raw emotional states. My work helped me develop an understanding of the conflicted loyalties many survivors of abuse felt, and how it often felt impossible for them to leave the relationship or give evidence against their abuser in court. Many women felt safer to 'side with the enemy' even when subjected to extreme violence. Other women clearly had very strong bonds with their abusers which didn't make sense to me – until I developed a deeper understanding of trauma bonding through my outreach work.

As an outreach worker, I provided one-to-one and group support to women. I began to understand common patterns of behaviour and thinking of women subjected to abuse. I saw recurring themes of confusion, self-blame, trauma bonding and inability to leave the relationship. When survivors properly understood that the abuse was not their fault, that they were not losing their minds and trying harder to please their abuser would not have helped, they would then have a very good chance of achieving real and sustained recovery. Because domestic abuse is intended to confuse, understanding patterns of abuse can be hugely validating and liberating for survivors. I saw the relief women felt and the progress they made when they properly understood what had happened to them.

In my outreach work with BWP, I often encountered women who were disappointed by police responses to their reports of domestic abuse. With a police background and an understanding of police processes and procedures, I was in a unique position to work with the police to improve their response to survivors.

In 2022, BWP was commissioned by Nottinghamshire's Police and Crime Commissioner to improve survivor experience and reporting of domestic abuse to the police. I was involved in this collaborative research project which identified key areas where communication could be improved. BWP's findings will hopefully encourage greater understanding by police officers and a more sensitive approach to domestic abuse survivors in future.

I have also been instrumental in improving processes within Nottinghamshire Police. I supported a woman whose former partner was on prison licence and who had a history of serious violence, particularly against women. He made a malicious allegation to the police that she had assaulted him. The police took his report seriously and unfairly cautioned her for assault, forcing her to give up her career as a carer because of this unjust criminal record. The police had failed to investigate properly and did not consider the full circumstances nor establish that she had been the victim of a campaign of serious and sustained abuse by the man. I forced Nottinghamshire Police not only to withdraw this woman's caution, but also to review its procedures for Out of Court Disposals. In highlighting this case and bringing about a review of procedures, other domestic abuse survivors should benefit from a fairer police investigation if they are the subject of malicious allegations by a domestic abuser.

Who is this book for?

This book is predominantly to help female survivors of domestic abuse by men understand what has happened to them. Women who have not suffered abuse but may enter a new relationship with a man will also benefit from reading it. Teenage girls who may have future relationships with men will benefit from gaining this knowledge. Abusive men who are determined to make positive changes in their behaviour may be enlightened by the book – change is possible if accompanied by very strong internal motivation. This book is written for professionals such as police officers, solicitors, social workers, doctors, nurses, midwives and teachers who will habitually encounter domestic abuse survivors during their work. Employers who want to support their female staff positively will also benefit from reading the book.

How to use this book

Female survivors can read this alone – the book is intended to de-mystify domestic abuse with a view to promoting recovery. It can also be used as a course book for group sessions – (The Survivors Programme: see website www.domesticabuses.com for more information). Whether reading it alone, or as part of a course, I strongly recommend keeping a journal. Journaling is not for everyone, but many people will reap huge benefits from the process, including self-discovery, finding inspiration, tracking progress, improving confidence and reducing anxiety. Journaling can be highly therapeutic and can help women work through difficult emotions and move forward.

In this book, I aim to provide readers with key information about men's abuse of women in an easily accessible format. From my work with survivors, I know that reading and understanding this material can bring about powerful and sustained positive change. I have added a case study to each chapter to make the material more 'real' to the reader.

Warning

It's not always easy to read about domestic abuse and you may find some of the contents of this book shocking and upsetting. The chapters on sexual abuse, physical abuse and using children to abuse might be particularly difficult for some readers. You can mitigate some of the stress you may feel by reading in an environment where you feel safe, reading small chunks at a time, and having a friend on standby to talk to as you work through the chapters.

There is also a risk that you might feel your experience of abuse is invalidated by reading this book. When survivors hear about or read of experiences that they consider more serious than their own, they commonly conclude that they're complaining about nothing and they will often minimise their experience. There will always be someone whose abuse was worse than yours, and it would be unlikely you'll relate to the abuse discussed in every chapter of this book. Please be aware of this and don't minimise your experience but know that every woman's experience of domestic abuse is different.

Acknowledgements

My sincere thanks go to the many women I have supported over the years. Our conversations have given me the expertise to properly understand domestic abuse. I am constantly inspired by your strength, perseverance and hope often in the face of terrible circumstances. I feel indebted to you for all that you shared with me. Please know that you have made it possible for me to write this book and in doing so, you must take credit for helping many other women recover from domestic abuse.

Why do Men Become Domestic Abusers?

"Of course I make all the important decisions, I'm the head of the household!"

"Men don't abuse women because society tells them it's ok. They do it because society tells them they are entitled to be in control."
– Hill, 2020[1]

Human behaviour is complex and it is never possible to prove cause and effect. However, there appear to be two main factors that contribute to men's abuse of women. First, that society has historically been patriarchal and in many ways remains so today – this gives many men the expectation of exerting power and control over women. Abuse is used to maintain this power and control that they see as their entitlement. Secondly, damaging childhoods involving poor parenting and trauma sometimes lead to narcissistic personality disorder, where behaviour is characterised by an inflated sense of self-importance, a need for admiration from others and a lack of empathy. These character traits are often associated with abuse in intimate relationships later in life.

The role of society

Society traditionally tells us that men are more important than women, more deserving of wealth, privilege, power, status and success. Hundreds of years of patriarchy has laid a solid foundation for this belief. Greek philosopher Aristotle wrote that women were "Inferior, incomplete, deformed versions of men." (Freeland, 1998[2]). There are countless other historical references that support this notion such as the delay in women getting the vote (1928 for over 21s). We might imagine that we have progressed since then but, although significant improvements have been made, we are still very much influenced by our history and there are many inequalities that remain today.

Historically, women have been given so few rights in law, they have effectively been considered the property of men, first their father and then their husband. When getting married, women were always 'given away' by their fathers in a symbolic transfer of ownership. Brides would promise to 'obey' their husband and always take their husband's name upon marriage. These practices can undermine women and perpetuate the belief that a wife is the property of her husband, and she should do as she is told by him. Though the law has progressed, this progress has been slow. Until 1992, forced sexual activity and rape were not unlawful within marriage, conferring on married men the right to sexually abuse their wives without regard to any question of consent – her body was his to do with as he pleased. Despite the law now being changed to make marital rape unlawful, it takes time for beliefs and behaviour to change. A report by the 'End Violence Towards Women Coalition' (2018[3]) found that a third of all adults believe sex without consent in long term relationships is not rape, we still live in a society that often demands women's subordination to men.

> *"We can't resolve the scourge of domestic violence or female genital mutilation without also taking on the societal norms that see women routinely spoken about, and to, as if they are second-class citizens whose sexuality exists solely to satisfy and be policed by men."*
> *– Bates, 2019[4]*

Men still get the top jobs

Despite women now attaining better educational qualifications than men, it is still men who secure a disproportionate number of top jobs. Even when employed in the same role, men will often be paid more – the gender pay gap remains an issue and demonstrates the continued inequality of opportunity that women have always been subjected to. Society still upholds the notion of men's superiority over women, that it is men who should hold the power and control. (Gracie, 2019[5])

Women are the subjects of sexist jokes

Women are also commonly ridiculed and are frequently the subject of sexist and misogynistic jokes. Jokes that sexually humiliate and suggest ignorance, stupidity, subservience and sexual availability are still often made against women – *"Women need to know that men have two emotions, hungry and horny, if you see him without an erection, fix him a sandwich."*

It's not just in jokes, women are also denigrated and humiliated in the media, film and the music industry, too – *"Slut you think I won't choke no whore till them vocal cords don't work in her throat no more."* (Eminem, 2000)[6]

Perhaps it's more subtle than in years past but evidence throughout society reinforces the notion of male supremacy. When society reinforces the belief that men are entitled to power and control over women, men feel their abuse of women is justified. Women will also come to believe this and accept their subservience. Women may also teach their children these expectations and 'role model' submissiveness in their intimate relationships.

The traumatic childhood

Although worryingly common, many men will not become domestic abusers despite being raised in a male-dominated society. A second and very significant risk factor appears to be a traumatic childhood which features attachment disruption. For healthy development, children require a safe emotional connection with a primary caregiver with caregiving being responsive to the child's needs. Secure childhood attachments lead to healthy cognitive, social and emotional development. These children are likely to develop empathy, have a capacity for love and be able to control aggressive impulses. Childhood attachment can be disrupted in a number of circumstances – childhood abuse, both physical and emotional, neglect and lack of responsiveness, and the sudden loss of a close attachment bond. Children traumatised in this manner may lack the ability to feel love and empathy, they may have poor self-esteem, narcissistic personality traits and may be unable to form secure attachments later in life. Not surprisingly, domestic abusers have very often suffered traumatic childhoods, often characterised by a lack of secure attachment.

Abuse, neglect and emotionally distant parenting that leads children to feel inadequate can also trigger the development of feelings of intense shame, sometimes known as toxic shame. Toxic shame is very different from healthy shame which is short-lived and helps teach us right from wrong. Toxic shame is felt long term. Shamed people feel inferior and exposed. Because the toxic shame is so painful and reminds people of their childhood trauma, they often replace the shame with anger, a less triggering emotion. People who behave in an angry manner when they feel shamed will often see shameful experiences as caused externally. If they assault their partner, rather than feeling guilt for behaving in that way, they are likely to blame their partner for causing them to resort to assault. If they verbally abuse their partner, they will likely believe she deserved it. If they make a mistake, they will not acknowledge blame but will blame someone else. These people will be hypersensitive to personal attack and will hide their shame with controlling tactics. Abusive behaviour is a major psychological defence to a host of insecurities often caused by poor parenting and trauma in childhood. Being angry, violent and controlling can mask desperate insecurity. Despite their bravado and apparent sense of self-importance, most abusive men feel broken, unworthy and deeply unhappy beneath their angry and controlling facades.

Poor parenting also gives rise to poor adult role models. Children will often copy parents' behaviour and if this behaviour is cruel, bullying and abusive, it's likely a child raised in this environment might become abusive, too.

Understanding that an abusive partner has been damaged by societal influences, dysfunctional parenting or past trauma can have a liberating effect on the survivor. She may finally understand that she really wasn't to blame for his behaviour despite having been repeatedly told she was. But there is a danger that this knowledge may elicit empathy in some women who may feel motivated to try harder to help him to overcome his demons. This is very often not possible if the trauma was intense and the coping strategies are deep rooted.

Whether acting out societal expectations of what is expected of them, or misbehaving to protect their vulnerable and fragile emotions, exerting power and control over their intimate partners could help abusive men achieve their objectives. When they dominate, undermine, blame, ridicule, belittle, degrade, assault and project they will experience a sense of control that they so badly need. If their partner shows signs of resisting their controlling tactics, the abuse will often escalate in an effort to re-establish control.

> *"A controlled child also learns that the default human approach to interaction is forcing, threatening, or manipulating others."*
> *– Cikanavicius, 2018*[7]

For whatever reason men feel the need to acquire power, the quest for power and control is at the root of the vast majority of domestically abusive behaviours. The actions of an abuser are almost invariably deliberate, controlled and targeted. If the issue was anger management and a lack of impulse control, these men might assault and abuse colleagues and friends, too, but they tend not to. There is a delicate balance to most domestically abusive behaviour; it needs to be well-managed, monitored and finely turned to work effectively. Very often, especially with more covert forms of abuse such as coercive control, men will try hard to keep their abuse subtle enough that it is not picked up on and challenged – just under the radar of conscious awareness so women imagine they're slowly losing their minds and don't understand why. This is why it is imperative to understand the reasons behind the abuse and the mechanisms of abuse in order to survive the experience of being abused.

As long as society sanctions patriarchy and children suffer trauma and neglect, domestic abuse will thrive.

Selina's Story

"I was drawn to Mike because despite his outer confidence, I could sense he was fragile underneath. In the early days, he confided in me about his childhood, it was brutal. His mother was the worst, she wasn't just neglectful, she was also cruel. His father was a domineering bully, dead now. Despite this, he still felt forced to visit his mother, she had some sort of hold over him and I could tell he was desperate to win her respect, her affection. She never gave it. I thought I could repair the damage of Mike's past, I tried so hard. When he was angry, this was often, I'd be understanding and would try to soothe him. I tried not to take things personally when he raged at me. I really believed I could make up for his mother's damage. I was wrong.

"Things got worse, it seemed as if the more I gave, the more abusive he became. We had a toxic relationship. I had counselling and came to understand that I was trying to change Mike, that what he was wasn't acceptable or good

enough, but I was trying to improve him and as I now know, and always knew really – people can't just change their personalities. With Mike, I can see now, the damage was done. Properly accepting he wasn't going to change and that I couldn't fix him made my decision to leave easier. The decision was easy, the leaving was horrendous – but I'm beyond the worst now. My advice to any woman at the start of a new relationship – if he's damaged by his past, you can't put that damage right and nor can you change him. Take a good long look at him and ask yourself, is he good enough for me as he is?"

Coercive Control

"You're always losing your keys; can you honestly not remember where you put them?"

What is coercive control?

Coercive control can be defined as an act or pattern of acts of assault, threats, humiliation, isolation, intimidation or other abuse that is used to harm, punish, frighten and control. Abusive men will often 'micromanage' every aspect of their partner's life, allowing her little choice or freedom. Coercive and controlling behaviour has been a criminal offence in the UK since the introduction of the Serious Crime Act 2015. However, there have been few successful prosecutions. It is an offence that is very difficult to prove because it often encompasses countless small acts that aren't witnessed outside of the relationship. It is also an offence that seems poorly understood by the criminal justice system. Broken jaws and black eyes are far easier for the legal system to understand and deal with. Coercive control is also difficult for the survivor because it undermines confidence and confuses. Women abused in this way may often believe they're in some way to blame for their abuse.

> *"Asking clients – 'Is there someone in your life making you afraid or controlling what you do or say?' promises an even more profound awakening than asking women about violence."*
> *– Stark, 2007*[8]

Ownership

Coercive controllers often believe they own their intimate partner's. Claiming ownership enables them to justify controlling every aspect of their partners' life. Normally a desperate insecurity drives their behaviour, a terrible fear of losing their partner and an obsessive need to prevent this from happening. Controlling their partner may give them a feeling of power that they desperately need to manage their own feelings of unworthiness. Coercive controllers are often highly jealous and possessive, but not always. They sometimes operate from the entitled belief that they have a right to protect their own property – their partner being their property as they see it.

Tactics used by coercive controllers

'Love bombing'
(Lavishing someone with attention to manipulate and influence them.)

A common tactic of abusive and controlling men is to 'love bomb' early in the relationship. Moving the relationship on quickly, declaring love early and being very intense in the courtship phase coerces women into believing their partner is devoted. It can be flattering but it is highly manipulative.

> *"I was intoxicated by his passion for me – he wanted and needed me so much and this made me feel very special."*
> *– Survivor*

The 'terrible childhood' and other sob stories

Earlier in the relationship, the terrible childhood or evil ex-girlfriend may be mentioned as a way of eliciting sympathy and excusing abusive behaviour. Women are often drawn in by these sob stories and want to do all they can to make up for his neglectful mother or abusive father. The terrible childhood is likely to be true; most abusive men seem to have had unhappy childhoods. Bad childhoods often create narcissists. Knowing this, their partner may feel motivated to be more tolerant of poor behaviour and try harder to show love and compassion to make up for his terrible past. She may want to prove she won't cheat on him like his ex-girlfriend (this probably isn't true), so she may go along with his need to monitor her movements and check her phone. She may excuse his terrible jealousy and isolation tactics. Many of the stories used to elicit sympathy are complete lies.

Isolating

Women are more easily controlled when isolated from support networks of family, friends and colleagues. Abusive men use a variety of methods to isolate – from sulking when their partner socialises with friends – being jealous around other men, to stopping their partner working, or being so rude when she invites family to the house that she doesn't dare do this often. An isolated woman is very vulnerable to manipulative and controlling behaviours, and she has no 'sounding boards' or point of reference.

Reinforcing traditional gender roles

"If you alter your behaviour because you are frightened of how your partner will react, you are being abused."
– *Horley, 2017*[9]

Expecting his partner to stay at home, care for children and carry out menial household tasks while he works outside the home is common amongst controlling men. He may claim to be 'head of the household' and, as such, make all the important decisions. He might give his partner endless lists of household tasks and get angry if his dinner is not on the table on his return from work. Behaving like this will reinforce his perceived superiority and close down his partner's options.

Name-calling, 'put-downs' and criticism

Once the relationship is established, abusive men may begin using criticism and 'put-downs' as a means of control. These criticisms and 'put-downs' are sometimes so subtle that the woman may not interpret them as being abusive – but even though she may not be consciously aware, her sub-conscious is likely to detect the criticism and make her feel terrible. This abuse can also be more obvious and will often focus on accusing the woman of being stupid or criticising her appearance.

"For most of our relationship, he referred to me as 'fucking stupid slag' or variations of this. It wasn't until I left that I fully realised how terrible this was and how much damage it caused me."
–Survivor

'Gaslighting'
(Manipulating another by psychological means to cause that person to question their sanity.)

Abusive men may 'gaslight' by questioning their partners' memories, denying events, trivialising their feelings, and misrepresenting situations to confuse and trick. This is an insidious form of psychological coercive control that makes survivors question their perception, judgement and sanity. It is highly undermining and women subjected to it might really believe they are losing their minds. A common gaslighting tactic is to hide her car keys and suggest she is losing her memory when she's searching for them.

Controlling access to money

Financial abuse is almost always a factor of coercive control. Once access to finances is controlled, women's options, particularly her ability to leave, are massively curtailed. In losing control of finances, women lose control of many other aspects of their lives.

Physical assault

Assault is often threatened and sometimes carried out. Coercive controllers may use assault and fear of assault to manipulate. Once his partner knows that this method of control might be used, he can give her subtle reminders such as a clenched jaw or an angry look to frighten her into behaving as he expects.

Abusive men may step up their coercive control if they fear their partner might leave

The cancer diagnosis

When men are worried about losing control of the relationship, they'll regularly claim to have cancer – this is very common and they will sometimes go to great lengths to embellish their claims by listing manufactured symptoms to their GP, who may refer them for further testing. Few women will feel able to leave when they believe their partner has a cancer diagnosis. Men may also purport to be in great pain and deliberately lose a significant amount of weight to help trick women into believing they are genuinely ill. They may tell their partner's family and friends who might encourage her to look after him. The terminal illness lie can prove impossible to walk away from.

Promises to change

When concerned that their partner might leave, abusive men may manipulate by admitting their real issues and making promises to change. These promises can be difficult to resist.

"I know I drink too much but I've checked in with AA, I'm doing this for you."

"I know I get angry, but I'll go for anger management, I can't live without you, I'd rather die."

"We can go for counselling together; I'll do anything not to lose you."

The reality is that even if they are intent on change, (but often they're not), domestic abuse is about power and control, and so addressing anger problems or challenging alcoholism will rarely stop the abuse. However, women are often drawn in by these promises of change and may be 'guilt-tripped' by the perpetrator if they consider leaving despite such promises.

Threats of suicide

Threats of suicide and suicide attempts are common actions of abusive men. Sometimes suicide is carried out. The terror of seeing a partner standing on a chair, a belt around his neck threatening to jump is enough to persuade most women that they need to do what they're told and give up the dream of fleeing the relationship. Even though he's making the threat against himself, the risk of a suicide attempt will be too appalling for most women to contemplate. It is the ultimate in emotional manipulation and a highly persuasive tactic. If there are children in the family, the threat of suicide will impact on them, too, adding an additional sinister dimension.

Threats to kill

But it's not just threats against themselves; abusive men will often threaten to kill their partner as a means of control, especially when there is a threat that the relationship will end. Sometimes there is a constant reminder – *"If you ever leave, I'll kill you."* At other times it's said when there is a real fear of losing control – if he fears his partner may leave. We know that domestic homicide happens all too frequently and that women are most in danger at the point of leaving, so it's no surprise that this is a highly effective and powerful threat, very likely to increase his control over his partner's behaviour. Women will know this won't always be an empty threat and the consequences of the threat being carried out are terrifying. When children are involved, they are regularly included in the death threats. Women are often capable of a high degree of self-sacrifice when they fear their children are in danger. They are often successfully persuaded to sacrifice their freedom and happiness by staying with the perpetrator if they believe this is necessary for him to withdraw his threat to murder the children. Threats to kill are so commonly made by abusive men that they feature on domestic abuse risk assessment forms. Making threats to kill is extraordinarily abusive and menacing, and also a highly effective persuasive strategy. Threats to kill are difficult to police. The threat alone does not constitute a criminal offence – it is also necessary to prove he meant the threat to be believed. Proving someone's intentions can be very tricky, so few prosecutions arise from these death threats.

Revenge porn (Sharing private sexual images of another without consent and with intent to cause distress.)

'Revenge porn' is an increasingly common form of abuse and the threat of having intimate pictures sent to family, friends and colleagues, or uploaded to the internet, is a powerful weapon used by abusive men. It is a criminal offence with a maximum prison sentence of two years, perhaps not long enough when the consequences for the victim are so profound. Just the threat of this is an act of intimate terror and likely to induce obedience in the survivor. Some men will quite deliberately obtain intimate images either overtly or covertly early in a relationship. By doing this, they possess a powerful means of manipulation, to be deployed as and when necessary.

Using children

Children are used by perpetrators of abuse in a variety of different ways to manipulate and persuade their partners. Abusive men will seemingly not care about the damage caused when they emotionally burden children as part of their abuse.

"Mummy doesn't love me anymore and I'm really sad and upset because I love her."

"Mummy wants to kick me out and I have nowhere to live and no money to buy food."

Putting children in this situation will have two advantages for the perpetrator: first, the children may try to influence their mother to behave as their father expects; secondly, she will be anxious to avoid this abuse of them, knowing what damage it is causing, and so may want to do what's demanded of her to save her children from further emotional harm. Threats may also be made to keep the children should she try to leave and, knowing how professionals are often persuaded and manipulated, too, this can be a very real threat.

Return of love bombing

The 'love bombing' that is often seen early in the relationship can be deployed again to target a woman threatening to leave. Protestations of undying love can be confusing and disorientating; claims that he's nothing without her and can't live without her can trigger empathy in survivors. This behaviour can take a more sinister turn when he tells her that if he can't have her no one else can or, if she leaves, he will always find her. These obsessive gestures of love mixed with abuse are alarming and frightening – they can cause the survivor to feel completely trapped and believe she has no options. This behaviour is likely to persuade the survivor to stay in the relationship and behave as she is expected.

Coercive controllers can be highly dangerous

A history of physical assault was considered to be the biggest risk factor for very serious assault or murder – the theory of escalating physical abuse. More recent research has indicated that it is the coercive controlling abusers who pose the greatest risk of murdering their partners.

A study published in 2021 of 358 domestic homicide reviews by Dr Jane Monckton-Smith[10], of the University of Gloucestershire, showed that control was seen in 92% of domestic killings, obsession in 94%, and isolation from family and friends in 78%. These types of behaviour can lead to a victim having no life of her own and no privacy from her abuser, who will frequently monitor her day and night.

Dr Monckton-Smith identified an eight-step pattern leading up to the killing in **almost all** the domestic homicides that she had researched. The eight steps were identified as:

1. A pre-relationship **history** of stalking or abuse by the perpetrator
2. The romance **developing quickly** into a serious relationship
3. The relationship becoming dominated by **coercive control**
4. A **trigger** to threaten the perpetrator's control – for example, when the relationship ends, or when the perpetrator gets into financial difficulty
5. **Escalation** – an increase in the intensity or frequency of the partner's control tactics such as stalking or threatening suicide

6. The perpetrator has a **change in thinking** – choosing to move on, either through revenge or by homicide
7. **Planning** – the perpetrator might buy weapons or seek opportunities to get the victim alone
8. **Homicide** – the perpetrator kills his partner, and possibly hurts others such as the victim's children. (Monkton Smith, 2021[10])

How coercive control affects women

- Depression, anxiety, stress.
- Feelings of helplessness and fear.
- Feeling isolated and being trapped in a toxic relationship.
- Experience of toxic guilt that accompanies self-blame.
- Low self-esteem and poor self-care.
- Being more vulnerable to mistreatment from others.
- Loss of employment and financial freedoms.

Tips for surviving the coercive controller

- Many men use coercive control tactics. If the abuse is not serious and there is no intention to leave the relationship, there are ways of managing this abuse and standing up to it. However, we are concentrating here on the more serious abuse that is not possible to live with or change.
- Understanding these persuasive tactics used by abusers can be the key to dismantling their power. When women know the games abusive manipulators play to trick or frighten them into behaving in

a certain way, the games lose some of their effectiveness and women can understand that they are not going mad. Education is key!

- Maintaining communication with friends, or other support networks where possible, is very helpful. Good friends can provide a more realistic perspective when you become confused and doubtful due to the abuse.
- Access professional support from a domestic abuse charity if you can. Someone with domestic abuse expertise will provide invaluable support because they will understand all the tactics to which you are being subjected. Having professional support can also help manage your risk.
- Standing up to an abuser and telling them you're leaving will threaten their feelings of control and encourage them to use more extreme tactics. This is why it is important to carefully plan your leaving the relationship and put a safety plan in place to mitigate any danger.
- Collect evidence of your abuse and record all instances of abuse. Do it safely – you must never be found doing this. Collecting evidence has various uses. You might wish to report the abuse to the police, if so, document your abuse and take photos of injuries, abusive text messages or emails etc. Also because coercive control is confusing and often leads to self-blame, writing about what has happened may give you clarity and a more objective perspective that is essential in helping you to recover.
- Journaling is a helpful tool for recovering from any form of domestic abuse.

Gemma's Story

"I'd wanted to leave for years; I was emotionally broken by Tom's control of me. He'd taken charge of every decision in my life. I didn't feel able to think for myself. I was confused about so much except for one thing – I needed to leave. Tom seemed to read my mind. The first time I properly contemplated leaving, Tom was diagnosed with prostate cancer – well, that's what he told me and I believed him at the time. I hadn't told him of my intentions, but he'd always watch me so closely and he must have guessed. I immediately realised I couldn't leave him with a serious illness and I committed to supporting him. He told me he had various hospital appointments and procedures, but there were no hospital admissions. He told me he was successfully treated but that it could come back at any time. I'm now pretty certain the cancer diagnosis was a lie.

"Two years later, I told him I was leaving. I knew he was having an affair, so I felt brave enough to tell him, imagining he'd be relieved. I was wrong. He became suicidal, and told me I couldn't do this to him, we were married, and I had no right. He never once said he loved me, it was as if I was his property and he wanted things to remain as they were – him having the freedom to do as he liked, me doing as he expected. Soon after this, I returned home to find Tom standing on a chair in the kitchen with my dressing gown cord around his neck. I was so shocked seeing this. I wanted to believe he wouldn't have gone through with it, but I felt terrible, and responsible somehow. I thought it was my fault for driving him to this – he told me it was. His antics bought him another year of my life.

The death threat came when I did leave. He didn't know where I was, I'd just collected a few essentials and fled while he was away for the weekend with his girlfriend. I had blocked him on my phone, but he rang from another number. He only said it once but so clearly and with such intention – "Gemma, you know this is stupid, you either come home today and it will be fine, if you don't, I will find you and kill you". My blood ran cold. He didn't find me so couldn't touch me physically but instead tore me apart on social media. He was calculatingly manipulative, accusing me of leaving him for another man, that he was confused and heartbroken. He claimed to whoever would listen that I'd been sleeping around for years, taking him for granted and controlling him. I lost friends who believed him. I have a new life now. I like to believe the death threat was a lie too, but I can never feel sure."

Isolation

"I lost everyone. In the end there was just him and me."

Abusive men may isolate their intimate partners

Why do they do this?

They do this because it helps them gain power and control. They isolate women from family, friends and sometimes work colleagues. They may also isolate their partners from access to professionals such as GPs, dentists and police, often when they fear abuse might be reported, or bruises seen and questions asked.

When isolated from support networks, women are more susceptible to abuse and more damaged by the abuse. Excessive jealousy and the desire to make their partners more vulnerable so they can exert power and control are two main drivers for the desire to isolate.

Excessive jealousy

Excessive jealousy is a common trait amongst abusive men, linked to their belief that women are their property and need to be sexually controlled. They believe that given the opportunity, women will go off with other men; they feel vulnerable and struggle to cope with the thought that their partner might leave them. Abusive men often have narcissistic traits, so beneath the confident façade they're often racked with insecurity and feelings of unworthiness – they cannot tolerate the thought of losing 'their' partner, 'their property'. These men might restrict women physically by locking them in the house. If they are allowed out, they might track their movements and interrogate any social contacts. They might turn up unannounced at their partner's workplace to check up on them. Sometimes it becomes impossible for women in this situation to continue to work. Abusers often control the clothing their partner wears and might ban make-up, always fearful that other men might pay attention. They may threaten physical abuse if the women does not do as she is told.

"He was madly jealous. I kept my eyes on the floor when we were out together – if I had eye contact with another man, he would rage at me. Leaving the house on my own wasn't an option."
– Survivor

Making women more vulnerable and easier to manipulate and abuse

Abusive men also isolate women so that they become more vulnerable and easier to abuse in the absence of social support. Isolated women can lose confidence and self-esteem and become more dependent upon their abuser. Isolated women also lose their sense of normality and will be less likely to realise that what is happening to them is wrong. They are often successfully persuaded to believe that the abuse is their fault. Perpetrators do all they can to weaken women in order to continue their abuse, and social isolation is a very effective way of breaking women down and adding to their vulnerability. Abusers may be sulky, non-welcoming or rude around family and friends, so that it becomes much easier not to invite them anymore. They may load their partner up with household tasks that are impossible to complete and have an expectation of dinner on the table on their return from work so there is no time to go outside the house. They often exert financial control. Without money, opportunities to socialise outside the home become limited. Abusive men may keep women pregnant, then refuse to help with childcare, thereby deliberately limiting their partner's freedom.

Family and friends will actively isolate the survivor

It's not only the abuser who is responsible for isolating survivors of abuse. What is less well understood is that family and friends will often 'freeze out' the survivor. It might seem surprising that survivors are isolated by family and friends, but this too is a common dynamic that adds to the survivor's distress. There are many reasons why family and friends turn their backs. Most commonly, it is because they become frustrated that the survivor is not leaving the relationship despite being **told** she must. Common phrases trotted out are: *"She's made her bed, so she can lie in it"* or *"I've told her to leave and she won't, I'm washing my hands of the problem" or "she keeps going back to him so in my mind she deserves what she gets."* Sadly, there is a common lack of understanding and a myth that a woman in an abusive relationship has a free choice to leave – if only it were that easy!

Friends and family negatively judge the survivor

When women are abused, they sometimes behave in ways their family and friends find difficult. This behaviour can lead to negative judgments and the severing of connections and friendships. Survivors will sometimes self-medicate with alcohol and recreational drugs; the abuser may force alcohol and drugs on her, too. When depressed and undermined by the abuse, she may lose respect for herself and her personal care. Women are sometimes not allowed by their abuser to provide good childcare and in some situations, particularly when they feel unable to leave the perpetrator, their children are removed from their care. When family and friends don't understand the dynamics of domestic abuse, they often judge negatively and distance themselves from the survivor, blaming her as a justification for their lack of support.

Bringing shame upon the family

If women leave the abusive relationship, they are often further isolated. Bringing shame upon the family is sometimes a reason for abused women to be 'cut off'. Some families believe divorce is shameful and think that women should stay in an unhappy marriage whatever the circumstances. They believe divorce will bring dishonour to the family and worry that this will reduce the family's social standing. When survivors who leave an abusive relationship have this family influence imposed on them, they often find themselves financially and socially abandoned by their families.

Abusive men manipulate family and friends against the survivor

Abusive men are often expert manipulators and will use these skills to abuse and isolate if their partner leaves. The family concerned with family honour and shame will often happily take the perpetrator's side with little persuasion. Other people will be influenced when he claims to be heartbroken and says he doesn't understand what more he could have done to demonstrate his love for her. He might go on a social media campaign purporting to be devastated by her abuse, suggesting she'd never been faithful and that he couldn't have tried harder for her. Women often don't discuss the abuse until they have left, so they are less likely to believed when they finally do talk about it.

Jealous friends

Many friends are not true friends. It's very common for some of the survivor's 'friends' to decide to side with the perpetrator when the relationship ends, particularly if he starts a social media campaign against her. The sad fact is that many people whose lives are less than perfect take joy from other people's distress. These 'friends' may listen to the survivor and then pass information to the abuser. They sometimes spread lies about the survivor and generally 'stir things up' to make trouble – then sit back and watch the fallout. This behaviour can come as a terrible shock to the survivor, who may then feel she cannot trust anyone. This situation is alarmingly common and can leave survivors feeling very alone.

The survivor's children may become hostile

The perpetrator will commonly 'poison' the children against their mother by telling them untruths, while overindulging them and setting no boundaries. When she's lost the support of her children and sometimes adult children too, the rest of her support network can quickly fall away.

Survivors of abuse will sometimes isolate themselves

Survivors themselves will often actively cut off social ties. Domestic abuse commonly leads to depression, anxiety and low self-esteem. Depression saps energy so that the effort required to maintain friendships can feel impossible. Survivors may lack motivation to maintain friendships even if 'allowed' to do so. Low self-esteem can make women feel unworthy of keeping their friends. If still living with the abuser, survivors will often keep friends and family at a distance, because they are not comfortable being seen with bruises or having others witness the reality of their difficult lives. Financial abuse is almost always a factor of domestic abuse – if access to money is restricted, survivors may feel unable to socialise with friends.

> *"I got to the point where I didn't want to go anywhere. I was depressed and I'd got out of the habit of making any effort for myself. Friends stopped bothering to invite me anywhere and I was relieved."*
> *– Survivor*

How social isolation affects women

When social isolation is so damaging to mental health and emotional well-being, it's no surprise that survivors of abuse suffer so much, and often continue to suffer long after the abusive relationship has ended. When suffering from fragile mental health in the aftermath of an abusive relationship, rebuilding severed social contacts can seem an almost impossible task. Human contact, including love, friendships, intimacy, family and a feeling of belonging, is a vital human need. The psychologist Abraham Maslow[11] theorised a 'hierarchy of human needs' (1954) and suggested that the need for social contact is so strong it can override the need for safety, as witnessed by children clinging to abusive parents. When the need for human contact is not met, people become susceptible to loneliness, social anxiety and clinical depression. This is seen very commonly in survivors of domestic abuse.

When isolated from access to appropriate medical care, dental care and other support services, physical and mental health can suffer further. Medical issues remain untreated and the survivor might become vulnerable to serious complications of treatable conditions. Survivors with pre-existing vulnerabilities or disabilities may be affected more seriously if unable to seek appropriate medical treatment.

Women who are prevented from continuing paid employment suffer the loss of contact with colleagues who are friends. They also suffer financial abuse and will lack financial independence. Financial independence allows freedom and this potential freedom is denied them.

Tips for surviving social isolation

- If you're still living with the abuse, do what you can to maintain at least one social connection. This person may need to be very careful around the abuser and not allow him to feel threatened by your friendship.
- If you've left the abusive relationship, you may need to audit your friendships and establish who your real friends are. Anyone who has shown sympathy for the abuser, or questioned your actions once you've explained the abuse, may not be a genuine friend. You can often establish who is a genuine friend by the feeling you get when in their company. True friends will make you feel validated, respected and valued, but if you are left feeling drained following contact, this person might not be a genuine friend.
- If friendships have dropped off because you've not been 'allowed' to maintain contact, do what you can to reconnect with lost friends. This can feel very difficult and it may take courage to reach out to these people; however genuine friends will be understanding and embrace the friendship again. If they don't, perhaps you are better off without them.
- If the abuser is 'trashing you' on social media following a relationship split, you have two clear choices. The behaviour might be serious enough that you could report harassment to the police, although sometimes repeated reports are needed before the police will take action. The other choice is to try to ignore what is happening and remind yourself that harassing and bad-mouthing in a public forum tends to reflect badly on the abuser rather than the person they're

attacking. Your true friends will know the truth and not be poisoned by such antics. This is easy to say, but more difficult to do. Try to care less about what people think and say about you if you can – it's liberating!

- Making self-care a priority will help you to re-build self-esteem that is often damaged during an abusive relationship. Looking after our emotional and physical health is likely to make us feel better about ourselves.
- Returning to work, if this has been denied, can be a positive step towards recovery. Employment provides much more than financial benefits – the social connections with colleagues and sense of purpose that employment can bring are also beneficial. Voluntary work or enrolling in courses may also help reduce isolation and provide a sense of purpose that might have been lost.

Jasmine's Story

"I left Tony five years ago with nothing and no one. Tony did everything he could to isolate me and get me on my own and he succeeded. The first thing to go was work and with it my colleagues. I resisted at first, but he persuaded me that he needed my help with his business and it was better for tax reasons if I was working for him. This wasn't what I wanted, but he manipulated and I eventually agreed when he left me with little choice. The reality of working for him meant doing a bit of admin from either his office with him or at home alone. Not only did I lose my colleagues, but I also lost financial freedom – I was never paid a salary of my own, and after the first six months I gave up asking for this.

"My friends fell off because Tony was jealous. He never told me I couldn't socialise, but he made things so impossible it was easier not to. If I saw my friends, he would spend the following week sulking. If they came to our house, he would be moody around them, and this made me feel uncomfortable, so I didn't like inviting them. To my family and especially my parents, he was charming. He seemed to be the perfect son-in-law – polite, respectful, successful, they were drawn in by him. My parents were always impressed by money and they saw Tony as a 'provider' which they liked. Before I left, I once tried to talk to my mother about how unhappy I was, but she refused to listen. She thought I wasn't appreciative and was expecting too much. I lost my family almost completely. The hostility I experienced from them was horrible. They didn't seem to care about what I wanted; it was all about causing shame to them – my feelings weren't important. Tony made things worse by siding with them to try to win me back. It was all about image with him – he didn't care about me, but he was enraged that I'd left and taken control of my life. I see my family a couple of times a year and it feels strained. I don't get invited to big family gatherings anymore and I understand why. Things haven't been easy since I left, but at least I have my freedom and with that comes new possibilities."

Sexual Abuse in Intimate Relationships

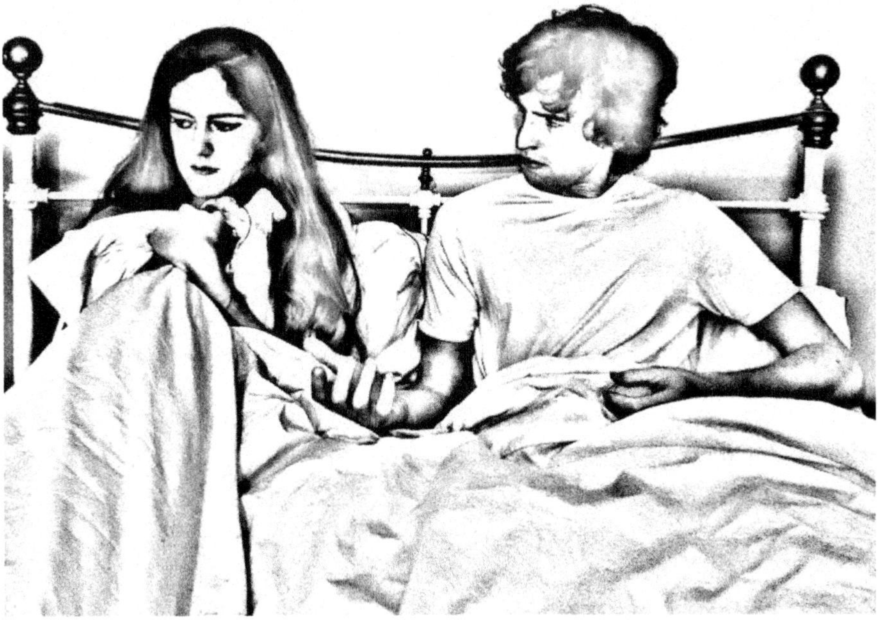

"It wasn't rape, I never refused, I wouldn't dare do that."

Sexual abuse is about power and control

Like all forms of domestic abuse, sexual abuse is about power and control first – sexual gratification is a side issue. Throughout history, invading armies have sexually abused and raped women, children and men, intended as a highly effective means of dominating, humiliating and breaking down individuals to gain power and control. Sexual abuse in intimate relationships is also used to degrade, humiliate, crush, subjugate, violate and render submissive so that power and control can easily be exerted. Because of the highly intimate nature of sexual abuse, its impact is particularly devastating for the survivor.

"Man's discovery that his genitalia could serve as a weapon to generate fear must rank as one of the most important discoveries of prehistoric times along with the use of fire and the first crude stone axe."
– Brownmiller, 1975[12]

Why some men believe they have the right to sexually abuse

The historical context of sexual abuse goes a long way towards explaining why some men believe they are justified in abusing women's bodies without any notion of the question of consent. Rape and sexual abuse in marriage only became unlawful in the UK in 1992. Prior to that, men could legally rape and perform forced sexual acts on unwilling wives who could do little to protect themselves. Men could claim their 'conjugal rights' – a term meaning rights to sexual intimacy within a marriage, which implies a lack of requirement to obtain consent. Decades after the law was changed, some people still believe that rape is not unlawful in the context of a long-term relationship.

Sexual activities do not need to be unlawful to be abusive; women have suffered for centuries because unwanted sexual acts have been forced upon them in intimate relationships. The fact that they had no protection in law arguably made their experiences worse – their feelings of horror, degradation and violation were completely invalidated by society. Being told to 'lie back and think of England' was a phrase commonly used to suggest to women that their duty was to make themselves sexually available to men, even when they didn't want intimacy.

Image based sexual abuse and revenge porn

Although sexual abuse in intimate relationships has always existed, its nature has changed in recent times, largely due to technological developments. 'Revenge porn' is a very disturbing development riding on the back of 'smart' technology. Private sexual photographs or videos are shared without consent, to cause distress to the subject of the photograph. This form of abuse is now frighteningly common and is a gendered crime with women constituting 90% of all victims. Abusive men will sometimes deliberately take images of their intimate partner early in the relationship, so they have material to manipulate and threaten her as and when they decide. Obtaining a naked or next-to-naked picture of another person gives you power over them. (Penny, 2015[13]) Educating women about the risks of making themselves vulnerable by allowing the images to be taken is not always helpful and it also constitutes victim blaming! These images are often taken covertly in the bedroom or bathroom with hidden cameras. Technology is a powerful weapon in the abusive man's arsenal.

"I stayed in the relationship for a year longer because of his threats of revenge porn if I left. In the end, I couldn't take it any longer and told him to do his worst – he didn't do it, but for that year, he controlled me with the fear of it."
– Survivor

Stealthing – a form of rape

'Stealthing' is an act of non-consensual condom removal during sex. Although condoms have been in common use for decades, this phenomenon was first discussed in 2017 by Alexandra Brodsky in The Columbia Journal of Gender and Law, (2017[14]). It is considered a sexual assault or rape because the condom removal is without consent and the consent to intercourse was conditional on its use. Stealthing sometimes has devastating consequences, including unwanted pregnancy and sexually transmitted diseases. It violates the sexual and reproductive rights of women. The reason behind the condom removal is not to increase sexual pleasure but is justified by men who practise it as a male right – a selfish act of power and control, the perpetrator feeling entitled to his partner's body, contempt for women and the belief in male sexual supremacy. Men discuss this crime on internet sites such as Reddit. In 2019, Lee Hogben was convicted of rape after stealthing a woman in a hotel room and was sentenced to 12 years imprisonment. Despite this, few convictions for this form of rape are secured.

Rough sex gone wrong

Abusive men use objects such as bottles and sex toys to inflict injury deliberately in intimate situations. Women are less likely to report intimate injuries to the police, so abusive men are more likely to get away with this form of abuse. If this abuse is reported, 'sex games' or 'rough sex' has sometimes been used as an excuse in British courts by abusive men to justify causing serious injuries to women. 'Rough sex gone wrong' has even been used to explain deaths of intimate partners. Abusive men have often claimed their partner consented to violence for sexual gratification in sadomasochistic-style sex. This form of sex has been normalised with the popularity of the films and the books in the 'Fifty Shades of Grey' series. (James, 2012[15]) The 'rough sex' defence was not officially a defence in law, but juries related to it and murder charges have been dropped in favour of manslaughter. In 2016, Natalie Connolly was killed by her boyfriend John Broadhurst after he caused 40 separate injuries. He said her death was due to a sex game gone wrong. On the judge's direction, the murder charge was dropped and he pleaded to manslaughter by gross negligence for failing to seek medical help. However, the new Domestic Abuse Act 2021 includes an amendment invalidating this defence when the victim suffers serious harm or is killed.

Non-consensual strangulation

Non-consensual strangulation may also be inflicted on women by domestic abusers during sex. This is a terrifying act that makes women fear death, but it tends to leave few signs of injury and has historically been punishable only as common assault. Strangulation is second only to stabbing as a cause of death in domestic murders therefore is seen as a 'red flag' for domestic murder. In the Domestic Abuse Act 2021, non-fatal strangulation has become an offence in its own right, giving women a level of protection they didn't previously have.

From rough sex, stealthing, non-consensual strangulation, and revenge porn, women are subjected to serious sexual violations, often at the hands of a man they know, trust and even love.

Abusive withdrawal of intimacy

Sexual abuse is not always physical. It sometimes takes the form of the withdrawal of sexual and physical intimacy. This form of abuse can be crushing for women and is designed to be so. Physical rejection of an intimate partner can lead to low self-esteem and feelings of worthlessness. Men will often express revulsion about their partner's body. This expression of disgust is often focused on the woman's vagina. Complaints are often focused on its size. He might claim her vagina is too loose to please him. Men will sometimes unfavourably compare women's bodies to those of porn stars. This type of abuse can have a devastating effect on a woman's sense of self.

"I never would have called it sexual abuse because he wouldn't touch me, he looked disgusted if he saw me naked. I internalised his disgust and felt terrible about my body, about myself."
– Survivor

Abusive demands for sex

More often, sexual abuse takes the form of insensitive demands for sex without regard for the woman's wishes. Women will commonly acquiesce to these demands because to do so may be the safest option. Sexual abuse is always accompanied by other forms of abuse and will never be a feature of an otherwise happy relationship. Women often make careful choices based on damage limitation, always mindful of their safety and doing what's required to avert an escalation of abuse. If women refuse sexual demands, they may be raped. If not raped, they may be subjected to name-calling or accusations that they're frigid, or their lack of interest cited as evidence that they're having an affair. Sometimes women are required to perform sexual acts to buy themselves privileges; they may be expected to pay with sex to be allowed out of the house to go to work. Women might be required to perform oral sex before being allowed out of the car to purchase food for the family.

Unacknowledged rape

Survivors of domestic abuse may be raped in their intimate relationship but fail to acknowledge that their experience constitutes rape. Unacknowledged rape can be defined as "an experience that meets the hallmarks of rape or assault but is not labelled as such by the victim. Instead, terms like 'misunderstanding', a 'hook-up gone wrong' and 'grey area' are used." (Thompson, 2021[16]) Thompson suggests that when rape is perpetrated by someone we know and love, it can be difficult to identify sexual violence when it's actually happening to you.

The impact of sexual abuse on women

Sexual abuse can encompass physical abuse, emotional abuse, coercive control and financial abuse (forced prostitution). Because of its intimate nature, this abuse often has a terrible impact on the survivor's mental health. Physically, sexual abuse can be particularly dangerous because injuries are often inflicted internally and strangulation can be a feature. Women may also be made vulnerable to sexually transmitted diseases. Emotionally, women often suffer trauma, depression, anxiety and feelings of low self-worth. Survivors are less likely to report this type of abuse and when they do, the police and judicial systems often subject them to an in-depth intrusion into their sexual history, which can create a secondary trauma. When men want to control women, sexual abuse is a highly effective strategy. Until society no longer tolerates men thinking that they should hold the power and control in a relationship and treating women as their property, sexual abuse will persist in intimate relationships.

Tips for surviving the sexual abuser

This is such a huge and complex subject; a few bullet points won't be of much use. In general terms, we should remember what we would tell our teenage daughters – your body is yours and you should never feel coerced, pressured or forced into sexual activities. Because domestic abuse and in particular sexual abuse, is so confusing, it's sometimes worth considering your feelings and gut instinct – if it doesn't feel right and you don't feel good, then perhaps you shouldn't be doing it and you might be experiencing abuse.

Women's response to sexual abuse varies hugely. Some can openly talk about being raped in their relationship with little apparent distress; for others, a similar experience will trigger intense trauma. Whether the abuse is current or historic, if it is negatively impacting you, it is advisable to seek support. The type of support needed will be determined by your level of trauma and it might be that specialist sexual abuse support or trauma support is needed. If the trauma is less serious and the sexual abuse not the main aspect of the abuse, then your local Women's Aid charity will be able to support you appropriately.

Julia's Story

"I didn't think that sexual abuse was what I was suffering, let alone rape! I just believed Stephan had a high sex drive. At the start of the relationship I was flattered, it felt like he wanted and needed me so much. Sometimes his demands were wearing, but I kind of felt it was my duty and I would feel uncomfortable saying no. He was exceptionally jealous and would get angry if he saw me speaking to another man. I was flattered by this at the beginning. He was always accusing me of wanting other men, so as the relationship progressed, I didn't dare refuse him sex because when I did, he became very angry and accused me of "shagging around." As time went on, I found his constant needs horrible. I resented everything about him and hated any intimacy. I wanted to end the relationship but didn't dare tell him. I struggled to hide my disgust of him. I did start refusing intimacy, I'd really stopped caring about the verbal abuse and I knew he'd never hit me. But he didn't accept my refusal and he forced sex upon me whatever I said. He told me I had no right to say no, I think he believed he owned me.

"I left Stephan five years ago. My life is so much better now, but I don't feel ready for another intimate relationship. I'm aware I'm still damaged by Stephan's abuse. I have major trust issues; I equate intimacy with abuse and can't seem to separate the two in my mind."

Narcissistic Abuse

"The person he was when we were out was very different from the monster he became behind closed doors."

What is a narcissist?

Narcissistic Personality Disorder (Lowen, 1997[17]) involves a pattern of self-centred and arrogant thinking and behaviour, a lack of empathy and consideration for others, an excessive need for admiration, and manipulative, selfish and demanding behaviour. Abusive men often have narcissistic personality traits. The type of manipulative abuse associated with narcissism can be highly damaging and is deliberately confusing.

Understanding this type of abuse can help women damaged by this behaviour to make sense of what has happened to them and can help others on the brink of entering a relationship to look out for warning signs.

Characteristics of a narcissist

- Fixations on fantasies of power, success, intelligence, attractiveness, etc.
- A belief that they are unique and superior
- Needing constant admiration from others
- A sense of entitlement to special treatment and to obedience from others
- Exploitation of others to achieve personal gain

- An unwillingness or inability to empathise with others' feelings, wishes or needs
- Intense jealousy of others and the belief others are jealous of them
- An arrogant demeanour

Why is he a narcissist?

Narcissists often have troubled childhoods. They may have been praised for what they have achieved rather than who they are. If they were shown love, this likely came with conditions. Narcissists have often experienced cruel and neglectful parenting.

When children aren't treated with empathy, they can stop trusting, start doubting themselves and develop a lack of self-worth. When children don't experience freely given love, they sometimes try to be special and better than others to fill the emotional void they feel inside. Behind the mask of extreme confidence lies a fragile self-esteem that is vulnerable to the slightest criticism. They decide they are better looking, more intelligent, more skilled – this pretence will help soothe their insecurities. They rely on others, particularly their intimate partner, to be complicit in their fantasy of superiority. The story of their troubled childhood and lack of love will often elicit sympathy in their partner.

Compassionate partners often show massive tolerance for terrible behaviour, reminding themselves that *"His mother didn't love him, no wonder he struggles sometimes."*

Common narcissistic behaviours fall into the following categories:

They 'gaslight' you

'Gaslighting' makes the survivor question their own sanity. The survivor may doubt themselves, lose their sense of perception and identity, and ultimately question their grip on reality. Abusive men will deliberately cause this feeling by lying, providing misinformation and falsehoods and questioning their victim's sanity to reinforce the damage they have caused. Survivors of gaslighting may find it difficult to make decisions and will question their judgement and decision-making.

Examples of gaslighting behaviour:

- Hiding items such as car keys and claiming she's 'losing it' when she repeatedly can't find things, expressing concern that she's suffering from early dementia.
- Claiming she's forgotten important information he gave her when he never gave the information in the first place.
- Seizing on any incident where she has genuinely made a mistake and using it as evidence that she's not coping and can't be trusted to manage.
- Tipping sugar in her casserole prior to the arrival of guests and behaving in a caring and concerned manner in front of the guests when she becomes confused as to how it happened.

They isolate you

Narcissists work hard to isolate their intimate partners. They do this because women will become weaker and easier to abuse when isolated from family and friends. Women will become more dependent and reliant on their abusive partner if social networks have been cut off. Insisting he can pay for everything so she no longer needs to work and telling her he loves her so much that they do not need anyone else around may be early isolation strategies. He may progress to being threatening and rude in front of her friends so they don't return again, or refuse to allow her out on her own later in the relationship.

They make you feel as if everything is your fault

Narcissists don't acknowledge blame and rarely apologise. They are hypersensitive to personal attack and will deflect blame for their mistakes or abusive actions onto others. It's common for the survivor to apologise for the narcissist's abusive behaviour and genuinely believe she's the one at fault: she may imagine it's her fault he lost his temper and said her cooking was disgusting; she might blame herself if he hits their child and may believe she should be stricter with parenting; and when she discovers his affair, his response might be to tell her she's useless at sex, so it's her fault. The survivor in a narcissistic relationship may believe that she just needs to show more love, try harder and stop being oversensitive, and things will be fine. This strategy inevitably won't work.

They control what you do and behave aggressively

Narcissists expect to have high levels of control over their partners and they use a variety of strategies to gain and maintain this control: for example, from physical violence and overt bullying to the more subtle strategies of guilt-tripping or introducing doubt and uncertainty to gain this control; and from holding a fist in their partner's face when she suggests seeing her friends, to questioning what her friends see in her, or sulking on her return so she is discouraged from seeing them again.

Disagreements are part of a normal relationship, but threats of violence, especially those used to control, are not. In a healthy relationship, both parties should feel able to disagree without fear of the other's reaction to the disagreement. With narcissistic abuse, it's common for the survivor not to dare question the perpetrator for fear of his reaction. Passive aggression is a more subtle form of aggression that narcissists use. They will sulk, fester, stomp off and act hurt in order to control and manipulate their intimate partners.

> *"Psychological abusers cannot feel love. They can only mimic what love looks like."*
> *– Thomas, 2016*[18]

They encourage you to be dependent

Narcissistic abuse will cause feelings of vulnerability in the target of that abuse. Narcissists work to systematically break down confidence and self-worth, so their victims feel unable to function on their own, by spreading negative emotions which make them feel powerful. They use phrases such as *"who would want you, you can't get anything right"* or *"you'd never find another man 'cause you're ugly and fat."*

There's often desperation on the part of the survivor to be good enough and to prove their worth, but the only person who can acknowledge their worth and make things feel better for them is the narcissist who, of course, will always cruelly withhold this validation.

They 'future fake'

'Future faking' is the term used for when the narcissist lies by promising things in the future to manipulate their intimate partner in the present. They may promise holidays and marriage with no intention of following through on these promises. They will make promises based on what they know will be very desirable to their partner. Narcissists very commonly over-promise and under-deliver with the sole intention of getting what they want in the present.

Narcissists create and project a false image

Narcissists tend to project a false and idealised image of themselves to hide their underlying insecurities. They want others to look at them with envy, admiration and acceptance and to view them as the dominant alpha male to be worshipped. Narcissists with gaslighting tendencies will boost themselves by marginalising those they perceive as weaker, often their intimate partners. They will attack their victims with overt or subtle cruelty and contempt, while gaining sadistic pleasure from this behaviour. They view interpersonal relationships, especially with their partner, as competitive rather than mutually supportive.

"Contrary to popular belief, narcissists do not love themselves or anyone else. They cannot accept their true selves, constructing instead fixed masks that hide emotional numbness."
– Lowen, 1997[17]

They use charm to manipulate

Narcissists are often particularly charming. They can be expert manipulators – friends and professionals can be persuaded that they are the caring, compassionate person they claim to be and the survivor is not always believed. Be very cautious around charming men!

"He's the charmer – the witty, confident, but overly controlling date."
– Sarkis, 2019[19]

They have control over their abuse

Narcissists are controlled and calculating with their abuse. Very different to the angry drunk, their abuse is the result of thoughtful planning, preparation and controlled delivery. They can choose to limit their abuse to threats of violence but stop short of punching their partner. They may behave in abusive ways that their partner might struggle to record as evidence. When the situation demands it, they can turn off their abuse and turn on the charm to manipulate the social situation in which they find themselves. If they gauge that their abuse has gone too far and their partner is at risk of leaving, they can pretend to be compassionate and caring until they feel they've recovered the relationship sufficiently to start abusing again.

The covert narcissist

Women may be fooled into believing their partner is not a narcissist, because he doesn't display the obvious signs of an overt narcissist who is characterised as being full of self-importance and may show off publicly. Another variation is the covert or vulnerable narcissist. The covert narcissist can present as withdrawn, anxious, self-critical, inferior, sensitive to the criticism of others and shy. They are often anxious, depressed and may display frequent suicidal ideations and self-harm. This outer presentation is misleading, the covert narcissist generally wants what all narcissists desire – admiration, a sense of importance and power and control over their intimate partner. Their tactics are often more subtle, his partner is likely to be very confused by the mixed messages he displays. Covert narcissists are typically chronically envious, lack empathy, are hyper-sensitive to criticism, can seem self-absorbed and may favour spending time alone. Their abuse may take the form of sulking, passive aggression, gaslighting, belittling and humiliation. They might appear altruistic in a public setting but cruel behind closed doors. Because of the subtlety of their tactics, survivors of the covert narcissist might be particularly conflicted and confused. They may be more vulnerable to self-blame and can find it very difficult to leave this type of relationship.

The silent treatment

The 'silent treatment' is an extreme form of passive aggression often employed by the covert narcissist. He may withdraw all communication and may even fail to give eye contact to demonstrate his dissatisfaction. It's a cruel form of manipulation designed to put the abuser in a position of control while silencing the survivor so that she is unable to assert herself. Attempts made by the survivor to communicate by any means are often met with contempt and silence. She may begin to feel that she doesn't exist and that she is utterly unworthy of her partners' attention.

> *"What I've learned through the course of educating myself on narcissistic abuse is that the positive behaviours offered by the narcissist are to actually enable the abusive behaviours to continue and eventually escalate."*
> *– Kozlowski, 2020*[20]

How does narcissistic abuse affect women?

- Anxiety, depression, and low mood.
- People-pleasing behaviours, especially towards the abuser.
- Low self-esteem and lack of confidence.
- Weak interpersonal boundaries – allowing others to abuse them, too.

- Attachment issues, being overly needy, especially towards the narcissist.
- Destructive behaviours including problems with addiction.
- Mental confusion and a feeling that there's something wrong with them.

Although it may include physical and sexual abuse, narcissistic abuse will often consist of countless small acts of emotionally manipulative behaviour. This behaviour is often subtle, intended to undermine and confuse, and over time it will leave the victim with self-doubt, confusion, anxiety, low self-esteem and a feeling that it is all their fault. The survivor can be left wondering whether they're imagining the abuse, are 'cracking up' or making a fuss out of nothing.

Tips for surviving the narcissist

- Educate yourself about narcissistic behaviour so you can understand why you've suffered. Read everything you can on the subject. Understand the cycles of abuse. This will help liberate you from the control that's been held over you.
- Set emotional boundaries (such as maintaining 'no contact' with your abuser) to make you less likely to be abused in future. These boundaries should be applied to all your social contacts, not just intimate partners. Decide what you're no longer prepared to tolerate – '*I won't make time for people who undermine me.*'
- Practise mindfulness and learn to live in the moment, especially when the past is troubling you.

- Practice self-care and self-compassion. Work hard to reclaim your true identity.
- Describe in your journal the narcissistic behaviour you've been subjected to, so you can understand how abusive this was and that it was not your fault that things were so bad.
- Acknowledge and accept that the abuse did happen and prepare to feel complex and difficult emotions.
- Try to get closure following the ending of the relationship. Because it won't be possible to have a reasonable conversation with your narcissistic abuser, you might write him a letter and then burn it or send it to him with no expectation of a reply, or only of an abusive reply. This helps some women.
- Seek professional help if you find recovery is difficult alone.

Sophia's Story

"Living with a narcissist robbed me of my life while I was with him. I was initially attracted to Muhammad because everyone else was. He was funny, good company, charming and good-looking. He made a real effort with his appearance, and I liked this. I felt flattered when he showed me attention. I know this sounds terrible, but I didn't think I was in his league, he could have chosen anyone. I fell in love very fast, but Muhammad drove the pace. I didn't feel ready for a marriage proposal two months into our relationship, but he was so persuasive that I agreed. Certain things were starting to worry me even then, but I dismissed them. I laughed at him once for putting odd socks on and he 'lost the plot'. He had an angry rage, accused me of 'fucking up the washing' and sulked for the rest of the day. I soon learnt never to criticise; he just couldn't deal with it. He'd also be moody and depressive when we weren't in

company. It was as if he became a different person when he wasn't showing off and entertaining. I felt it was my fault for not being interesting enough for him, I committed to trying harder to make him happy.

"After our wedding, my whole life seemed geared up to doing what he expected of me and trying to make him happy, or at least keep him calm. I failed most of the time. I told no one how bad things were. I didn't want to admit it to myself because I thought it was my fault he wasn't happy, that I couldn't make him happy."

Domestic Abuse and Self-Blame

"He could never blame me as much as I blamed myself."

It's normal for domestic abuse survivors to self-blame

Most women self-blame for the abuse they suffer in a toxic relationship. It's almost inevitable to some extent. Despite this being normal, self-blame can have terrible consequences – it may stop you leaving or slow your recovery if you have left. To fully recover and move on more positively, it's essential that you drop this self-blame. It's not healthy, it's not fair and it stands in the way of the self-compassion necessary to rebuild confidence. Being abused is not your fault!

He calls you a mental slag, terrorises you, monitors your phone, withholds money, isolates you. You will know this behaviour is abusive and wrong, but on some level you may feel it's partly your fault that he behaves like this. Your fault that he loses his temper, your fault he's having an affair, your fault you didn't try harder. If you'd only been more giving, shown more patience and loved him more, perhaps things would have been different.

There are lots of reasons we blame ourselves for being abused. We may have just one or many different reasons for thinking the abuse is our fault. As with so much in life, education is key. When we fully understand the reasons for self-blame, we can work towards freeing ourselves from this destructive thinking and know that the blame lies fully with the abuser.

These are the common reasons women blame themselves for being abused

He was lovely at the start of the relationship. Remembering this can make you think that this was his true personality. You may worry that it was you who triggered him to change his behaviour, that there was something in you that brought out the worst in him. You may have had previous failed relationships so you think that you're incapable of maintaining a good relationship. The fact is that abusive men need to make an effort early in a relationship because if they are unpleasant from the start, they wouldn't attract anyone. When remembering the good times in the early stages of a relationship, we tend to think his early behaviour was his true personality. This is not the case. Abusers are not capable of being kind and loving long-term. The seemingly loving man he played at the start was partly an act. It's not your fault that he became unpleasant, he always had an unpleasant side to him.

> *"He said we were soulmates, he was amazing, I always blow it with relationships."*
> *– Survivor*

He isn't horrible all the time. Few men are abusive the whole time. The common pattern is to chop and change between apparently caring behaviour and abusiveness. This is disorientating and confusing. You so badly want to believe your partner is not a monster, it is frightening to think he is, so you're inclined to believe that his nice side is his true character and that when he's abusive, it's your fault you have triggered this reaction in him. When you're invested in the relationship, you will deliberately excuse his unpleasant behaviour. He will tend to blame you for his anger and you will often accept this blame willingly. You may prefer to believe you have caused his aggression than believe you're in a relationship with a horrible man.

"But he can be so lovely, he can be really caring, I just need to work harder to make him feel loved."
– Survivor

He is happy with another woman in his subsequent relationship. Seeing your abuser in a seemingly happy subsequent relationship may reinforce feelings that you were to blame for the relationship failure and this thought will hurt very deeply. If you're in a trauma bond with your former partner, seeing him apparently happy with someone else will feel even more terrible. The reality is that it's either early days in his new relationship and the abuse hasn't started yet, or the new relationship is abusive but not obvious to anyone observing from the outside. Abusive men rarely change their behaviour and if they've been abusive in one relationship, they are very likely to behave in a similar way in the next. Just because it's not obvious, doesn't mean abuse isn't happening.

He's told you so often everything is your fault, you've ended up believing this. Blame is a common tactic used to undermine women in toxic relationships. It can lead to anxiety, depression, and lowering of self-esteem. When subjected to blame on a habitual basis and then suffering the consequential lowering of self-belief, we are more likely to accept the blame and believe it really is something lacking in us that triggers his behaviour. He will also blame you for his own mistakes because his self-esteem is too low to accept fault and apologise. You will often believe him and accept this blame and internalise it.

He's hypersensitive to personal attack and blames you for always attacking him. Abusers can't tolerate criticism and will perceive it even when it's not there. They feel fragile and vulnerable under the 'mask' they wear. This vulnerability puts them on the lookout for perceived attack. When we've been told so persistently that we're nagging, criticising and attacking him, we may believe this and blame ourselves for being critical and controlling. You will be 'treading on eggshells', worried about saying the wrong thing, unaware that you are the victim of his abuse.

He's incapable of accepting blame for his actions or apologising but will blame us for his abusive behaviour. Abusive men will blame us for triggering their abuse. We may be accused of 'winding him up' causing him to rage at us or told 'look what you made me do' after he has assaulted us. He will generally project his blame onto us. When our confidence and self-belief is eroded by the abuse, we may accept this blame and not question it.

We challenge him about his abuse and he projects his faults onto us making us doubt ourselves. Projection is a defence mechanism: it refers to taking unwanted emotions or traits about yourself and attributing them to someone else. If you are brave enough to challenge his abuse, a common pattern will be for him to 'turn the tables' and make out that you are the aggressor and he is the victim. He may tell you you're controlling, that he's 'treading on eggshells', that he was confident before he met you but now he's always scared of saying the wrong thing. This response to a challenge is common and can be confusing and disconcerting.

He's manipulated and 'gaslighted' you, so you question your judgment. (Gaslighting is manipulation by psychological means, so you doubt your own sanity.) Domestic abuse can be very confusing and it is often intended to confuse. The intermittent rewards, changing between nice and nasty with no apparent reason, can leave you feeling disorientated. What confuses even more is the gaslighting behaviour can be so subtle you don't detect what is happening. From the classic hiding your keys and feigning concern for you that you're losing your memory, to more subtle tricks that cause you to question your sanity, this behaviour corrodes you. When you believe you're going mad, losing your grip and can't be trusted to get basic things right, you will be easily persuaded to believe it is your fault when he becomes exasperated with you.

He's isolated you from family and friends. They might have provided you with a more realistic perspective and encouraged you to see that the blame lies with your abuser. Being isolated can encourage women to entertain irrational thoughts about their abuse and chronic emotions such as anxiety, guilt and shame get worse.

You're depressed, anxious, have low self-esteem and don't feel you deserve better. Domestic abuse can damage the mind as well as the body leaving survivors with depression, anxiety and low self-esteem. When damaged in this way, we are less likely to defend ourselves and more likely to accept blame. We can internalise this blame and genuinely accept his abusive behaviour is our fault. Low self-worth encourages us to lower our emotional boundaries and believe we don't deserve better. If we don't recover from these feelings, we are also more vulnerable to entering another abusive relationship.

He elicits sympathy from you for his difficult past and you blame yourself for not being compassionate enough. Domestic abusers have often had terrible childhoods and dysfunctional relationships with abusive parents. He will often use his past to excuse abusive behaviour and women often get drawn into forgiving too much and treating him with compassion and understanding despite his unpleasantness. As time goes on and the abuse intensifies, you may become less tolerant and less accepting of his excuses. He may use his past to guilt-trip you and tell you that you're just like his parents and no one can understand what he's been through. When you have naturally high levels of empathy, this can be difficult to hear and you are likely to blame yourself for not being patient or understanding enough.

We blame ourselves that we had an affair. It's not uncommon when in an abusive relationship, especially when physical intimacy is withdrawn, to seek love and validation elsewhere. It's a basic human need to feel loved and fulfilling this need can be seen as a survival instinct. Whether or not your abuser discovers your affair, you will often be filled with guilt that you took this action and fail to acknowledge the context which forced you to satisfy your need for emotional comfort.

We blame ourselves he had an affair. When you're told you're useless, stupid, ugly and no good in bed, you may view his affair as evidence you weren't good enough to keep him. When your self-esteem is corroded and you lack the confidence you once had, you may believe you deserve to be rejected in this way.

You leave the relationship because of the abuse and feel it's your fault for splitting the family and depriving the children of their father. This is a common reason for self-blame. Leaving a relationship when you share children is always a difficult decision to make. What you need to remember is that living together in a toxic and abusive relationship can be damaging for children too, and does not provide them with a healthy role model. Abusive men will often use the children to emotionally manipulate and intensify your feelings of guilt.

You may self-medicate with drugs and alcohol and blame yourself for these addictions. It is not uncommon for women to self-medicate in this way to deal with the trauma of abuse, although this behaviour generally makes the situation worse. If we drink too much and abuse prescription or non-prescription drugs, it is likely we will be blamed by all around us, including our family, friends and professionals, this will exacerbate self-blame. If we struggle with addictions, this may be a normal response to our trauma and we need compassion including self-compassion, not blame.

Toxic self-criticism. This is particularly common when the survivor has suffered serious trauma in childhood. Negative self-talk can be almost constant with women telling themselves they're worthless or not good enough. This becomes exacerbated when additionally abused by an intimate partner and in serious cases can lead to self-harming behaviours.

Your family and friends are often manipulated by him against you. It's not uncommon for family and friends to sympathise with the perpetrator. Women often don't disclose the abuse they are suffering in an intimate relationship when they're invested in the relationship and ever hopeful things will get better. They often disclose the abuse at the point of leaving. He may play the part of the devastated victim who feels broken at your rejection of him. Your friends and family may sympathise and blame you for being self-centred and cruel. When blamed by those closest to us, it's difficult not to accept this blame.

He has manipulated the children to side with him and blame you. It can be quite common for abusive men to manipulate the children against their mother. When our children blame and criticise us, it's likely we will feel as if we've failed them and blame ourselves too.

We live in a victim-blaming society. It's the norm for society to victim-blame. The focus is often on what the victim did to invite this behaviour. Victims of rape are questioned about their short skirts, sexual pasts and drinking habits. Men will often elicit sympathy following domestic homicide by talking about the killing being a 'crime of passion' because his girlfriend left him for another man. When it's so common to question what the victim did to trigger this abuse, the victim herself may well ask the same questions and be left concluding she was partly to blame.

"Victim blaming of women is prevalent and normalised in society. What causes us to blame women who have been abused, raped, trafficked assaulted or harassed by men? Why are we uncomfortable with placing all of the blame on perpetrators for their crimes against women?"
– Taylor, 2021[21]

As we can see, there are so many factors that encourage us to blame ourselves in an abusive relationship that most women will do this. Thinking like this is very destructive. It's important to liberate ourselves from self-blame.

How does self-blame affect women?

- Women are more likely to stay in abusive relationships when they self-blame. They don't leave because they believe they are the problem.
- Self-blame damages a woman's confidence, self-esteem and sense of self-worth.
- Self-blame can make women feel exceptionally guilty when they have children who are suffering from exposure to domestic abuse. This guilt is misplaced and damaging.

- Women are less likely to protect their children by reporting child safeguarding concerns when they believe they are to blame. They may fear that their children might be removed from their care.
- Women are less likely to report abuse to the police or try to protect their freedoms and rights when they suspect they're partly to blame.
- Women are more likely to accept abuse in a subsequent relationship if they don't accept that the abuse they were subjected to was in no way their fault.

Tips to overcome self-blame

Open your eyes to how he has treated you. Write things down to get a more objective perspective and ask yourself, 'Is his behaviour acceptable?' 'How would you feel if your daughter was treated like this by a boyfriend?' 'Would your friends put up with this behaviour?' 'Is his behaviour towards you unlawful in any way?' 'How does behaviour like this make you feel?' When you write things down it can help you to gain a more objective perspective.

"Becoming fully aware of the dynamics of psychological abuse is not an easy truth to absorb."
– Thomas, 2016[18]

Educate yourself about domestic abuse so you can understand how his behaviour fits into common patterns used by perpetrators of abuse. Understand that he is a domestic abuser and there can never be a valid excuse for this type of behaviour. Realise that he behaves like this to gain power and control over you.

Self-reflect to understand how various qualities you have may have led you to be highly compassionate despite his abuse. You may have high levels of empathy that made you very tolerant. Learn how these feelings are no longer appropriate, so you can be liberated from feeling sorry for him.

Understand his manipulation and 'gaslighting' behaviour and realise that he deliberately caused you to become confused and emotionally fragile so that he could dominate and blame you.

"Resist remaining in any level of denial. The truth is painful to see, but necessary."
– Thomas, 2016[18]

Build your emotional boundaries and write a list of behaviours you will no longer tolerate in anyone. For example, 'I will never be intimate with someone who calls me names', or 'I won't engage in a relationship with someone who wants to monitor my movements'.

Learn to be more assertive and practise these skills. There are plenty of online resources that teach assertiveness. When we are assertive, we will be less tolerant of abuse by others. We will have the skills to communicate our needs and utilising these skills will enhance our self-esteem. We will be less likely to blame ourselves for the poor behaviour of others.

Improve your confidence and self-worth. The way we treat ourselves is critical in this process: when we are aware of our inherent value, this shows on the outside too and encourages others to treat us well. When we value ourselves, we are less likely to blame ourselves for the behaviour of others.

"Read any news story today about domestic violence homicide and you're likely to see some version of the question, why didn't she leave? What you almost surely won't see is why was he violent."
– Snyder, 2020[22]

Seek professional help for domestic abuse. Talking with friends can often help, but they may not understand domestic abuse like professionals and will often fall into habits of victim-blaming or telling you how to think and what to do. Domestic abuse professionals will be able to talk with you about your specific circumstances, to help and guide you to understand that being abused is never acceptable and is certainly never your fault.

Although it can be difficult and take time, you can move on positively following domestic abuse. It's not likely that this will 'just happen' though. Self-reflection, reading about the subject and accessing professional help is often needed. Domestic abuse is not a simple process, it can take time to suck you in, is intended to confuse, so extricating yourself will take time and effort.

Although no one would choose to be abused, when you recover you will gain insight, strength and resilience that you previously did not have. Knowing that abuse wasn't your fault is an important step forward towards your recovery.

Amanda's Story

"I honestly believed it was my fault that he left me for my friend. I was filled with guilt that I hadn't given him enough, that I hadn't been good enough for him, that I was a complete embarrassment to him. I didn't realise at the time how abusive he was. I thought he lost his temper because of my stupidity – I couldn't get anything right, I embarrassed him in front of his friends, I never looked good enough and I was constantly getting things wrong. The more mistakes I made, the less I trusted my judgment. Because I didn't trust myself, I relied on him too much and when he wasn't happy with me, I felt destroyed. I honestly thought I was losing my mind. I doubted every action I took and became neurotic about messing up. He reminded me on a daily basis I wouldn't cope on my own, and then he left me! I felt devastated, humiliated and worthless. I also had a terrible feeling of guilt that he'd invested so much in our relationship, but I'd never really made any effort. This is what he told me and I believed him. I'd been so capable and happy early in our relationship but thought I'd just let myself go, both mentally and physically.

"Having sought professional help, had counselling and read extensively, I now understand his narcissistic behaviour. Because he never physically assaulted me, it didn't occur to me he was being abusive. I now understand his gaslighting behaviour, always changing the rules so I was set up to fail, deliberately confusing me, jumping on mistakes I made and highlighting them. I have suffered terribly, but I now feel

liberated knowing I was not to blame. I have lost the crushing guilt I felt for not feeling good enough for him. I know it was his abuse that wrecked our relationship and wrecked me for a while. Understanding this I now have every chance of recovery."

Financial Abuse

"If I didn't do as he demanded, he'd keep hold of my debit card until I did."

"Wealth means power: the power to subdue, to crush, to exploit, the power to enslave, to outrage, to degrade."
– Goldman, 1970[23]

What is financial abuse?

Financial abuse involves controlling a person's ability to acquire, use and maintain financial resources and it is almost always a feature of domestic abuse. Financial abuse is used to punish, trap, isolate, manipulate, humiliate and control women – it is an insidious form of coercive control that restricts women's freedom. Some men believe they are justified in controlling money on behalf of women – there are historic references they can rely on to support this belief. Until the Married Women's Property Act of 1882, women were required to give up all rights to their property to their husband upon marriage. For most of recorded history, men's pay has tended to be higher than women's. (Heather and Paci, 1998[24]) Men are sometimes paid more for similar jobs. Television presenter Samira Ahmed took the BBC to an employment tribunal in 2017 for paying her a sixth of the amount they paid presenter Jeremy Vine for a similar role. The employment tribunal concluded gender discrimination was the reason for this pay gap.

The gradual creep of financial abuse

As with other types of domestic abuse, financial abuse generally creeps into the relationship gradually. By insisting on paying for meals, the man is reinforcing the gender stereotype that suggests men control the money. By accepting this, women are acquiescing to a stereotype. By driving a bigger car and expecting his partner to drive the 'run-around', men are further reinforcing their financial dominance. Men may make grand gestures with lavish spending early in the relationship to suggest that they can pay for everything and that their partner no longer needs to work. He may say he can take care of her, that she doesn't need to worry about money. He may encourage pregnancy and giving up her job. He may pay her an allowance or housekeeping money to encourage financial dependence. Before long, women may find themselves trapped, with no job and little economic independence. Once in this vulnerable position, he may also further manipulate and abuse through his control of finances.

Sabotaging employment

Sabotaging work is one of the key ways abusive men undermine their partner's financial independence. Insisting on a pregnancy and then refusing to help with childcare so she is forced to give up her job is not uncommon. He may bully and intimidate his partner to stop working, threatening physical violence if she refuses to stop. He may deny her access to a car or money to pay for transport to work. He may ply her with drugs or alcohol, so she is unfit for work in the morning and forced to leave her job. He may bruise her face or blacken her eyes with punches, so she is too humiliated to turn up to work. Once employment is lost, so is a great deal of financial and social freedom.

"His toxic jealousy caused me to abandon my career. Any form of contact with men wasn't allowed. When I gave up my job, with it went my financial independence – my world closed in on me."
– Survivor

Control tactics

Controlling and abusive men use various tactics to deliberately damage their partner's finances. Abusers will often put assets in their name and liabilities such as bills in their partner's name. They may run up large debts on joint accounts, force their partner to work in the family business without pay, refuse to pay bills in their partner's name to ruin her credit score or apply for credit in their partner's name and fail to maintain the payments.

He may insist on remortgaging the house so he can buy himself a new car, or spend money intended to pay rent or important bills on other purchases. He may insist that she cashes in her pension so he can squander the proceeds on gambling.

Abusers will sometimes steal their partner's money, taking money from her purse or transferring it from her bank account to his. He may expect her to pay for everything while spending his own earnings on extravagant treats for himself. He may sulk when his partner buys items for the children, so she feels forced to buy him presents, too. He may financially exploit his partner by insisting she works while refusing to do so himself but controlling her earnings. He may sell her belongings, including jewellery and precious items, without permission to generate cash for himself. She may be able to do little to stop this behaviour when she is intimidated by his bullying.

Link with sexual abuse and addictions

Financial abuse is often linked with sexual abuse. Many sex workers are forced into this role by abusive partners intent on making money. Abusive men will sometimes pacify their partners with drugs before forcing them into sex work because they are more malleable as addicts. The abuser may keep a percentage or all of his partner's earnings. Once working in this role, further manipulation and control is possible – the abuser can threaten to report his partner to the police or expose her employment to family and friends.

Even within the relationship, sexual and financial abuse can overlap. Women are sometimes forced to perform sexual acts on their partner before they are given money to buy family food or children's clothing. They may also be 'rewarded' with money for luxuries following sex. Women controlled like this will feel desperate and degraded.

Addictions can exacerbate domestic abuse including financial abuse. Research suggests that there is a significant relationship between problem gambling and perpetration of domestic abuse. (Dowling, 2014[25]) Men with a gambling habit, particularly a pathological addiction, are likely to pose a serious threat to their intimate partner's finances. Online gambling is so readily available that it is sometimes possible to keep this habit a secret, especially when the abuser controls the finances. The survivor may not be aware until debt collectors move in. Addictions to drink and drugs create a similar threat to finances and due to the disinhibition caused by these addictions, the threat to the survivor can be intense.

Poverty

Women suffering financial abuse can find themselves in situations of serious poverty even when there is plenty of money in the household. It's not uncommon for women in these situations to rely on food banks and charity shops when they and their abuser earn a good income. When lacking basics including food, mothers will often sacrifice their own needs and put their children first. Domestic abuse often leads to feelings of low self-worth and with inadequate clothing and food, self-neglect can develop, causing further damage to the survivor.

"We had a nice four-bedroom house and Mark drove a new BMW. To the outside world we appeared wealthy, but my reality was very different. I wondered from one day to the next how I'd afford to feed the children."
– Survivor

Using divorce and financial settlement

If the relationship ends, divorce, financial separation and child maintenance provide further opportunities for men to abuse financially. Abusive men will commonly stop paying towards child support and housekeeping as soon as the relationship ends and if their partner has no employment, she may be left financially destitute. Abusers deliberately drag out divorce proceedings, hoping to force their estranged wife to pay the maximum solicitor fees possible. They may refuse to complete financial disclosures for the same reason. They may complete financial disclosures dishonestly, failing to disclose various assets. Child maintenance may not be paid, or earnings may be hidden so they do not pay what is due. Some abusers give up their jobs to avoid paying child maintenance.

Using child-related issues

Even when divorced and financially separated, financial abuse will often continue when there are children from the relationship. Abuse around child maintenance payments is often on-going, with men generating ever-creative methods of avoiding paying for their children. They will commonly claim that the children are staying with them more than they are in order to reduce payments due. Especially when self-employed, they may fail to disclose earnings to reduce the amount paid in child-maintenance.

Abusers often enjoy wasting the mother's money and will deliberately 'lose' items such as school shoes and uniform, forcing the mother to replace these items on a frequent basis.

Loss of power

> *"The abuser either gains overt or covert control over the household income. When this occurs, basic needs start to become scarce, even where the income levels do not warrant living in poverty."*
> *– Thomas, 2018*[26]

Controlling money is often equated with holding power and in domestic situations this is very true. When the abusive man controls the finances, his partner who is financially deprived loses power. Loss of employment will not only cause loss of financial independence but can also make her vulnerable to social isolation. Even if 'allowed' out, she may lack money to socialise with friends, causing friendships to drop off. Becoming dependent on her abuser for money for basic items, she will find herself at the mercy of his abusive and controlling demands and it will be easier for him to manipulate her. Financially deprived and possibly with children, too, she may have few options to escape.

How financial abuse affects women

- Lack of financial autonomy is the main reason survivors feel unable to flee an abusive relationship. This can happen to apparently wealthy women too, when they are unable to access their money.
- Freedoms, possibilities and options are lost when finances are sabotaged.

- Loss of employment caused by domestic abuse can lead to loss of skills and confidence making it more difficult for women to re-enter work at a later stage.
- Low self-esteem, anxiety and depression are additional side effects of financial abuse.
- Women may feel unable to provide adequately for their children and this can cause significant distress.
- Serious financial abuse can leave women with insufficient money to eat adequately. This can negatively affect their health.

Tips for surviving the financial abuser

- When in debt and financial crisis, it's common not to want to face up to dealing with the problem. If you've escaped a financially abusive relationship, it is very likely you may be in serious confusion over your financial situation and the extent of your debts because of the deception of the perpetrator. Your post may have been intercepted over a significant period so that you may not have access to details of your debts and this may seem frightening.
- Do what you can to assess the damage. Check your bank statements and collect all details of assets and debts. Try to establish what has happened with your finances. Get a credit report if you can.
- You may feel tempted to borrow from family and friends, take out 'payday' loans or use pawnbrokers to generate money to get by – don't do this, it will make things worse.
- Consider reporting fraud to the police. There may be enough evidence to progress an investigation but even if not, it can be helpful

to have police crime numbers because this adds credibility if, for instance, credit cards are taken out in your name and you claim that you shouldn't be liable for the debt.

- Seek professional help – it's essential. Much can be done to clear debts and build financial independence. Citizen's Advice Bureau (CAB) debt advisors will provide free support and guidance. Other providers such as Pay Plan work free of charge, often negotiating with creditors to get debts written off. Government schemes such as Individual Voluntary Arrangements (IVAs) help those with unmanageable debts to get part of the debt written off so they can then make manageable repayments.
- Make peace with what you have lost if you're unlikely to get it back. This can be difficult but it's essential for recovery. Women will particularly blame themselves when their children have suffered financial hardship. This is not your fault and if you can mentally let go of the losses and the misplaced guilt, you will be free to recover.
- Overcoming financial abuse is not just about sorting out your finances. You will also need to recover from the emotional impact of the coercive control and other forms of abuse you've been subjected to. But there is now hope for a better future. Don't suffer alone – access the support that's available to you.

Ruby's Story

"I'd been an independent woman making my own money and managing my own finances, to being controlled by my housekeeping budget. Sam's control crept over me, taking

away every last bit of independence that I'd had. Sam encouraged me not to return to work after our first baby was born. Encouraged is a generous word – he made it clear that he wouldn't help with childcare, so returning wouldn't have been manageable. After I'd used all my savings buying food and basics for our baby, I suggested we set up a joint account. Sam wouldn't consider it but said he'd pay me a 'housekeeping' allowance every month. I resented this, but Sam intimidated and scared me so I didn't feel able to argue. My budget wasn't big, but it was enough to manage on. Three months into this new system I realised he'd paid me £50 less. I questioned this and he listed a string of what he said were my failings that month. These failings included giving him eggs on toast when I was too tired to cook a proper meal and for failing to remove cobwebs from the hall ceiling. I was horrified and tried to encourage him to be reasonable, but he said he didn't expect to argue, all he needed were high standards from me and I'd be paid the full amount next month.

"It became difficult to maintain 'high standards' when I was exhausted from caring for our baby without help and I lacked an adequate budget to do a proper food shop. I tried very hard to manage and my efforts paid off when I was rewarded with a full housekeeping budget the following month. It's evidence of how controlled I'd become that I'd felt a rush of pride at having secured the full budget. This pride didn't last long. Withholding sex cost me £30 the following month, overcooked chicken another £10. I don't think I've had another full budget, despite trying so hard to do everything expected of me.

"I'm still trying, and if I work hard and do everything I can to keep him happy, I sometimes only have a tenner deducted. I feel trapped, I feel I've lost everything, I need to get away, but I'm exhausted."

Physical Abuse

"I tried so hard to keep him happy but nothing I did was ever good enough for him."

Physical Abuse

Physical abuse can be described as a deliberate or reckless act or omission that causes, threatens or might cause physical harm to the survivor. Men are almost always physically stronger than women and so any physical abuse or the threat of it can be very frightening and potentially highly dangerous. Physical abuse doesn't just take the form of assaults – it can also include withholding medication, denying hospital treatment and plying the victim with drugs or alcohol. As with other forms of domestic abuse, physical abuse is carried out for the purpose of gaining power and control over the survivor. Because of its frightening nature and potentially serious consequences, physical abuse is a highly effective means of controlling women in a domestic setting.

Indirect physical assaults

Indirect assaults are very common – men often feel safe in the knowledge that they can deny intention to assault. When they hurl the remote control or a glass at their partner, they may claim they had no intention of it hitting her. They may also feel one step away from the cause of the injury, as if causing the injury indirectly makes it more difficult to blame them.

Threats of physical assault

Threats of physical abuse can be highly effective as a means of control. Whether he's assaulted her in the past and threatens that he could do it again, or even when no previous assault has occurred, the threat of assault can be terrifying and will have the effect of making women do as he demands. Threats of physical assault can be very subtle, from a glance that only the survivor will notice to a clenching of the jaw. Or they can be more obvious – he might whisper in her ear *"wait till I get you home."*

Punching holes in walls and doors is a terrifying spectacle for a woman to witness. Again, this is a more indirect act but at the same time a highly menacing way of demonstrating his rage, especially when in close proximity to his partner. He wants her to see his power, know his rage and feel the terror. What he is communicating is that he really wants to punch her but that he is controlling this drive, so punching the wall instead. The hole in the wall or the door hanging off its hinges will serve as a reminder to his partner to do as he expects.

Pretending the assault was an accident

Pretending the assault was an accident is a common form of physical abuse. From ramming into his partner when he walks past her to tripping her over near stairs, or even pushing her down a set of concrete steps and insisting she just tripped. Scalding burns caused by a hot cup of tea are also easy to inflict. These forms of assault can lead to very serious injuries but proving intent might be difficult. Whereas women tend not to sustain black eyes accidentally, they do trip over, fall down steps and sustain burns. A coercive controller may successfully persuade her that it was just an accident, that she tripped rather than was shoved. Abusive men are often very creative when inflicting physical injuries that could have been caused accidentally.

Holding partners hostage

Holding partners hostage is a form of physical domestic abuse. Jealous men who fear their partner might leave the relationship may physically restrict her movements by locking or barricading her in the house. In more serious cases, women might be physically tied up. Men will also be motivated to do this to allow time for physical injuries to subside if they fear their partner may report abuse to the police.

Hidden injuries

Abusive men sometimes carefully inflict their injuries in a very controlled manner so the injuries are not likely to be seen by others. Hidden injuries are also less easy to prove should the survivor report the abuse to the police. Hair pulling can cause significant trauma, loss of hair and bruising but little, if anything, will be visible. Punches to the back of the head will be largely hidden. He may also choose to cause injuries to areas normally covered by clothing.

Visible injuries that cause isolation

Injuries such as black eyes or split lips can be inflicted without caring who will see the injury. These types of injuries are also inflicted to imprison women in the home. A black eye may take a couple of weeks for the bruising to subside, and in this time, the survivor may not feel able to see anyone, go to work or even leave the house. Women with significant visible injuries have felt forced to give up their jobs when they don't feel able to turn up at work with a bruised face.

Physical injuries caused during sexual abuse

Survivors of domestic abuse suffer terribly when sexually abused. While most discussion on the subject centres around the psychological and emotional harm caused by this form of abuse, the physical impact of sexual abuse can be significant. When women are raped by their intimate partner, especially when intercourse is rough and forced, vaginal injuries such as abrasions and tearing are common. These types of injuries can cause considerable pain, although there may be little to see in terms of visible trauma. Women with intimate injuries are less likely to report this abuse to the police because they often feel embarrassed. Abusive men sometimes inflict more serious intimate injuries with the use of objects including sex toys.

We also know that escalation of domestic abuse is often triggered by pregnancy and childbirth. Abusive men will sometimes demand intercourse too soon after childbirth and, in doing so, cause significant vaginal injury or injury to caesarean wounds. In extreme circumstances, they will force intercourse before the vagina has healed following stitching, leading to physical trauma, infection and a risk that injuries caused by birth trauma won't heal properly.

Deliberately infecting a partner with a sexually transmitted disease is a form of sexual abuse as well as physical abuse. This form of abuse can be devastating for the victim and may make her less likely to leave the relationship because she feels stigmatised by the condition.

Non-fatal strangulation is a physical assault that is often, but not always, inflicted during sex. This is a terrifying assault that often leaves little or no sign of injury, but the survivor may fear death. Until recently, it could only be dealt with as a common assault at most. Now this injury has been included in the Domestic Abuse Act 2021 as an assault in its own right.

Rough sex gone wrong has been used by men as an excuse for causing serious injury or the death of their partner. Men have claimed that rough sex was consensual – judges and juries have accepted this and been sympathetic so that men were given very lenient sentences. However, the Domestic Abuse Act 2021 has been updated to establish that no death or serious injury can be defended as 'rough sex gone wrong'.

Forced alcohol and drug abuse

Drugs, both prescription and illegal, and alcohol are sometimes forced upon women by abusive men. Women become easier to control when subdued in this way. A coercive manipulator can use his partner's drug and alcohol abuse to his advantage in many ways. He may use it to undermine her to professionals, use it to claim she's a bad mother and generally weaken her both physically and emotionally.

Physical vulnerabilities and health-related abuse

Assaulting a woman with physical vulnerabilities or pre-existing health conditions is an insidious form of abuse. Women with underlying health conditions will be more vulnerable to physical abuse, particularly if their abuser is also their carer. Abusers may particularly exploit vulnerabilities – they are sometimes able to cause significant pain and damage without leaving obvious marks. From twisting arthritic fingers to shoving a partner with a bad back, the damage caused may be significant but the visible signs of assault will be minimal.

Abusive men may deny their partners the medication prescribed to treat health conditions. They might also abuse by controlling when and how their partners take their medication and this can bring about serious health consequences.

Denying access to medical care is not uncommon, particularly when men fear assault injuries might be noticed and questions asked by medical staff. Women might not be allowed to seek treatment for significant assault injuries, so the impact of the abuse can become much more serious than the original trauma. When broken bones are not adequately realigned and set, or internal haemorrhages are left untreated, serious complications can arise.

Men who control might not allow women to seek medical treatment for health conditions not related to physical assaults. They may also prevent them from attending routine health checks such as mammograms or cervical smears. This abuse can have catastrophic consequences if cancers remain undiagnosed. It can also lead to serious consequences when more common and treatable conditions are left untreated. While antibiotics should quickly cure cystitis, denying treatment could lead to life-threatening sepsis.

Poisoning and controlling fluid intake

Abusive men sometimes cause physical damage by denying their partner adequate food or water, which can lead to serious health implications. They might also introduce poisons or force their partner to consume rancid food to induce food poisoning.

Justifying physical abuse

Abusive men will commonly believe they are entitled to control 'their' woman and if other forms of control fail, feel that physical abuse is justified. Men may also blame women for causing them to be physically abusive. Women might be blamed for 'winding him up' or 'pushing his buttons'. He may excuse his abuse by saying he has a 'short fuse'. Men often claim to have anger management problems but this is rarely the case with domestic abuse. If men had anger management problems, they would be violent indiscriminately and would attack others, not just their intimate partner. Men will claim drink made them violent but again this is an excuse for domestic assault, which is invariably calculated and controlled. As is usual with domestic abuse, men can rely on historic references to excuse their abuse. Under common law it used to be legal for a man to chastise (physically assault) his wife in moderation. Times may have changed but we still live in a society that often expects women to be subordinate on every level.

> *"I can't tell you how many abusers I've heard bemoaning their inability to stop loving the same women they assaulted so severely it landed them in prison."*
> *– Snyder, 2020*[22]

How physical abuse affects women

- At worst, physical abuse causes death. Death is not just the consequence of serious, direct assaults. Withholding medication, plying partners with drugs and preventing access to necessary health care can also result in death.
- Physical abuse can cause serious life-changing injuries.
- Physical abuse and fear of abuse can induce terror and lead to post-traumatic stress disorder (PTSD), where the survivor might experience flashbacks, sleep disturbances and mood swings that re-live the terror caused by the abuse.
- Other aspects of women's mental health may decline when subjected to physical abuse. Depression and anxiety are common outcomes.
- Women are controlled through physical abuse and the fear of it, losing many freedoms.

- Isolation is common in women subjected to this abuse. They are often isolated by the perpetrator but may also choose to isolate themselves if they feel shamed by the abuse they suffer.
- If women don't feel safe enough to leave a violent partner, they may risk having their children removed from their care.
- Women subjected to sexual physical abuse might suffer long-term problems with sexual dysfunction caused by physical and psychological trauma.
- Physical abuse can induce stress-related health conditions, such as irritable bowel syndrome (IBS), digestive problems and chronic pain.
- Women with disabilities can be even more vulnerable to physical abuse and the impact may be more serious due to their pre-existing health conditions.

Tips for surviving physical abuse

Staying safe Always be mindful of your safety and that of your children. Be aware that at the point of leaving and after you've left, the risk to you is likely to be heightened. Do not tell your abuser of your plans to leave. When planning to leave a physically violent relationship, seek professional support from a domestic abuse charity if possible. You will need a safety plan in place. You might be helped to flee to a refuge. You will be the expert at understanding your abuser and what is likely to trigger his aggression, so do what you can to keep him calm when still living with him.

Reporting physical abuse to the police You might not report the first incident of abuse. You may be abused on several occasions before first reporting, this is normal. If you do report abuse, don't just report the recent incident but the whole history of abuse you've suffered. You should record all injuries by photographing them. It can be good to have injuries documented by your GP, especially if they are significant. Write notes of instances of all abuse either in note form or on a word document – make sure your abuser never finds this. You need details including time, date and what happened. There is an app called Bright Sky where you can record abuse safely. When you do feel able to report the abuse to the police, you will have all details of abuse to hand, which will help with your statement. The police should keep your original notes to produce in court; this will add credibility to your evidence. Keep details of evidence in the form of texts and emails of admissions, abusive texts and emails, and ripped or bloodied clothing. Reporting abuse to the police can seem difficult, some women will decide not to, but if the abuse is serious, this is probably your safest option.

Whether you're still living with the abuser or have left, tell someone you trust. Keep at least one line of communication open. Seek the support of a domestic abuse charity if possible. You're likely to recover better with support. Much can be done to protect you and help you. Most importantly, you will be supported to re-build your self-esteem which is invariably damaged by domestic abuse.

Rachel's Story

"I tried to hide my injuries from everyone because I was ashamed. I couldn't bear for anyone to see me with black eyes or red marks around my neck. Ed knew this so he didn't care where he hit me. I felt ashamed because his abuse made me feel worthless. Other women didn't get treated like this, other women wouldn't tolerate this, but I did – this made me feel pathetic and inferior. My friends had said they would walk if a man ever laid a finger on them. They never saw my injuries because I stayed at home. I couldn't face their judgment. I was very hard on myself, in weak moments thinking I somehow deserved his abuse. I lost my job because I was off sick too often. I couldn't tell the truth. I spent so long trying to cover my bruises, but they'd just show through, makeup didn't work. I couldn't see my GP for a sick note so when the bruises hadn't faded enough after a week, I had to give up work. No one checked up on me or asked me why. None of my colleagues kept in touch, but to be honest I'd withdrawn from them, I'd lost my confidence for socialising.

"Everything came to a head when my neighbours called the police. This had happened before and I'd successfully persuaded them everything was fine, but not this time. My eye was in a mess and my nose broken, blood everywhere. Ed decided to fight the police too. They had it all recorded on their body cams. He was arrested and kept yelling, "The fucking bitch deserved it." I refused to give a statement. I was too scared, couldn't face court, didn't dare say anything against Ed.

The police were kind and tried everything to persuade me, they wanted to video interview me and play my evidence via video-link in court, but I just couldn't. I don't think they understood what fear feels like. As it was, they did an 'evidence led prosecution'. Essentially, they decided they had enough evidence without my cooperation. I was still scared. I felt I'd failed. I hadn't managed to persuade the police it was an accident. In my mind I repeatedly apologised to Ed.

"Ed was convicted and sentenced to seven years for GBH. There is also a lifelong Restraining Order stopping him from contacting me so I will have some protection when he's out. I can't stay here though. I'm awaiting a housing move to another area.

"I've had a lot of support and worked hard on myself since then. It's difficult but I'm in a better place than I was. When I was in that situation, my overwhelming feelings were fear, shame, lack of worth, and the need to protect Ed. I wanted to show him I wasn't the person he was accusing me of being, that I was on his side despite everything. It probably makes no sense if you're on the outside looking in, but at the time, protecting Ed was the only way I felt I could stay safe. If he could only see how loyal I was, maybe he wouldn't need to hit me, was what I thought. I've learnt to be kinder to myself, it's not always easy but I'm always working on it."

Stalking, Harassment and Electronic Monitoring

"I lost all privacy, every move I made was monitored."

"Every breath you take, and every move you make, every bond you break, every step you take, I'll be watching you."
– Sting, 1983[27]

What is stalking and harassment?

Despite there being no legal definition of stalking, the police and judicial system have adopted the following description – 'a pattern of unwanted, fixated and obsessive behaviour which is intrusive. It can include harassment that amounts to stalking or stalking that causes fear of violence or serious alarm or distress in the victim'. Stalking is interrelated with harassment and intimidation, and it is very often a feature of domestic abuse, particularly when the abuser is intensely jealous or following the ending of an abusive relationship. Men stalk their intimate partners or former partners as a means of exerting power and control over them. It can be a terrifying form of abuse and has serious consequences for a woman's mental health.

How men persuade women that monitoring them is okay

Early in a relationship, abusive men may insist on driving their partners everywhere and collecting them. He may insist on driving his partner on the pretext of 'just wanting to keep her safe'. He may phone several times a day saying it's because he loves her so much. FaceTiming is more intrusive, but he may say he loves to see his partner's beautiful face when he's at work. He may connect his phone to hers via live location, saying it helps him to know where to collect her. He might turn up at her place of work, saying he wanted to deliver her lunch. This behaviour may not seem abusive; some of it in isolation might not be and some women may feel flattered by this attention. It can be difficult for women to develop an understanding of what is normal when popular culture equates morbid jealousy and stalking with romantic love. (Snyder, 2020[22]) However stalking can easily escalate to more sinister forms of monitoring.

How men stalk, harass and monitor women:

Smart technology makes stalking easier. Developments in technology have given stalkers many more ways to monitor their partners. Spyware apps can easily be installed onto phones, laptops and tablets so that the abuser can access all data and traffic on their partner's device. Mobile phones can be cloned easily (a copy made of SIM card), so there is no privacy for the survivor when using her 'phone. Cyberstalking also includes sending harassing or threatening electronic or online communication. Social media platforms such as Facebook and Twitter are used to unnerve, threaten, harass and embarrass. This type of communication may also be used to disclose intimate or embarrassing information, or to carry out revenge porn. Stalkers often use a combination of physical (in person) and electronic monitoring, tracking and harassment.

Abusive men might be open about their monitoring. Some abusers will stalk and harass quite openly. Women may be required to 'phone in' several times a day so their abuser can keep checking on them while he's at work. Women may be expected to produce receipts as proof they've been shopping. Sometimes CCTV will be installed within the home so he is able to monitor her activities when he's out of the home and make sure that she doesn't go out. By doing this he will keep her electronically imprisoned.

Stalking and monitoring might be secretive. On other occasions, the electronic surveillance might be covert, such as checking her mobile phone when her back is turned and installing spyware on her phone or laptop so he can read her messages. Using hidden cameras and recording devices is a common trend, and these devices are increasingly smart and easily affordable.

"Oh, can't you see, you belong to me?"
– Sting, 1983[27]

Stalking and harassment can be intensified following the ending of a relationship. When an abusive relationship has ended, particularly when a woman initiated the ending, the abuser will very often step up his stalking and harassment, often with the intention of destroying the survivor's reputation by making disclosures about her on social media that might embarrass and humiliate. He may allege that she's mentally ill, or that she's been cruel, unfaithful and a bad mother. He may try to win over her friends and family by persuading them that he is the victim.

Some friends and family seem easily persuaded to side with the abuser – this is quite common and adds to the survivor's distress, encouraging her to believe she is to blame. Posting intimate photos is also common. Hacking into her social media accounts to cause trouble might be easy when he has access to her passwords. Abusive men might also want to revive the relationship. They will often harass by bombarding women with phone calls, WhatsApp messages and emails. Often, they intermittently vary their behaviour, one day promising undying love, the next day sending hostile messages and death threats. Women will sometimes choose not to block their former partner from contact. They understand that a careful balance is needed to keep themselves safe. If they block all contact, two issues arise – first, women fear that if they block phone contact, he will be more frustrated and may come to her door. She may also decide not to block him because she may feel the need to monitor his anger and persistence. By blocking him she may have little clue about his frustration and this can be frightening. Secondly, if she wants to report harassment to the police, by blocking him she will cut off her ability to collect evidence against her abuser. Deciding on the best strategy can be a difficult balance, but survivors are normally experts at keeping themselves safe and will generally know what the best action will be.

The Stalking Prevention Act 2019 introduced a Stalking Prevention Order (SPO). This is a civil order, which can be obtained by police from a Magistrates Court. This allows an early intervention by the police when there is as yet insufficient evidence to start criminal proceedings. It can also be used if a suspect has been charged as part of prosecuting a stalking offence. Although this is a civil order, it carries a criminal conviction if a breach occurs. Despite this new legislation being available, relatively few orders currently are sought by the police.

The impact of stalking and harassment on women

The impact of stalking and harassment on survivors is often profound. This type of behaviour typically triggers intense stress, low mood, hypervigilance, fear, feeling vulnerable and self-blame. Stalking will trigger disruption in the victim's life, from the need to change phone numbers and jobs to relocating their home. More serious psychological injury is common, including PTSD (Post Traumatic Stress Disorder), sleep disturbance, depression and inability to concentrate. The psychological trauma often caused can continue for years after the stalking has ended. Some women never feel completely safe again. However, with proper support, much can be done to protect the survivor from this intrusive and frightening behaviour and help her regain her confidence and feelings of safety.

Stalking by an intimate partner or former partner should always be treated seriously. It indicates an unhealthy and unnatural obsession and can be a significant risk factor for serious harm.

Tips for survival if you are being stalked and harassed

- Record instances of abuse, but do not let the perpetrator know. Keep emails, screen shots of messages, details of unwanted calls, photos of recording devices found and evidence of spyware installed.
- Report stalking/harassment to the police. If the police do not pursue the matter initially, do not be put off, but continue to collect evidence and report subsequent incidents.
- Consider obtaining a Non-Molestation Order (a civil order prohibiting the abuser from various behaviours). If breached, this becomes a criminal offence with up to five years imprisonment.
- Tell others who may be able to help keep you safe – your employer, neighbours, friends and family.
- Ensure your home is secure and take steps to increase your safety, for instance installing a CCTV doorbell. Ask your council if they can help you to secure your home. Councils will often offer help with changing locks and fitting more secure doors, this help is not restricted to council tenants.
- Increase your safety outside the house – carry a personal attack alarm, be accompanied by a friend and alter your routes.
- Do not let your stalker emotionally isolate you – rely on good friends to help you through the trauma.
- Remember you are the expert on knowing how best to keep yourself safe.

- As with all forms of domestic abuse, seek support from a local Women's Aid charity and consider counselling to help you recover.
- Contact the National Stalking Helpline on 0808 802 0300.

"Every move you make, and every vow you break, every smile you fake, every claim you stake, I'll be watching you."
– Sting, 1983[27]

Technical tips for survival if you suspect you are being electronically monitored

- Prevent your abuser from having physical access to your phone. It takes seconds to link your phone to theirs via live location and less than five minutes to download a spyware app.
- Password-protect your phone and devices and don't share the password with anyone.
- If you feel you're being tracked, turn off the location settings on your phone.
- If you think spyware may be installed on your phone or other devices, preserve the evidence by reporting it to police or by taking a screenshot of the spyware app if you've identified it. You can download various scans to check for spyware. If identified, methods for removal vary depending on the type of phone or device you have. A Google search will provide comprehensive instructions. If this fails,

a factory reset of the device will normally remove spyware. If in doubt, seek professional help.

- If you believe your phone has been cloned (a copy made of your SIM card), you will need to change your SIM.
- If you believe your mobile phone handset (IMEI) has been cloned, you will need to change your handset, but this is far less common than a cloned SIM.
- Do not click on suspicious or unverifiable links in emails or chat messages. A click can trigger the silent installation of a tracker or spyware on your smartphone or laptop.
- Change your passwords on a regular basis and be careful about your privacy.
- If you are worried that your home/bathroom/bedroom may have bugging devices, a Google search will provide comprehensive information on how to check and deal with these. If still unsure, seek professional help.

Ebony's Story

"I'd been in a relationship with Gavin for only two months when I decided to end it. He was too intense, obsessive, and what started off feeling good ended up freaking me out. The real problems began when he wouldn't accept I'd finished with him – he wouldn't take no for an answer. He bumped into me when I was out with friends and joined our group and acted as if we were still together. I was embarrassed and angry too. This happened a couple more times, in different settings and I couldn't understand how he always seemed to know where I'd be. Gavin started posting pictures of us together on Facebook with love heart emojis. This made me scared for the first time

because I realised he was obsessed with me. I tried to ignore what was happening and get on with my life, but this proved difficult. He messaged me several times a day telling me he still loved me and wanted to restart our relationship. He pleaded with me; it was awful. I ignored his texts and then blocked him. Following this he started ringing me from various different numbers. I blocked them too when I realised, but I became scared not knowing which calls were safe to answer. I considered reporting him to the police, but I feared this might make him angry.

"Three months after the end of the relationship, I went away for the weekend, driving two-hours to Blakeney in Norfolk. I felt relaxed and less anxious. I'd switch my phone off or leave it in the hotel room. I felt safe. The second day there, I saw Gavin's car in the car park – not him, just his car. I was terrified. It was then I realised he must be electronically monitoring me, it suddenly made sense. I headed straight home; the holiday was wrecked.

"I reported his abuse and the police took it seriously, I wondered why when they were clearly so busy. I now know Gavin was well known to them and had a lifelong Restraining Order relating to a former girlfriend. He was arrested and the police downloaded his phone. They had to seize mine for evidence too. What they found horrified me but no longer surprised me. They confirmed he had cloned my phone so had access to all data on it – my text messages, emails, everything! They also discovered he had intimate pictures of me that he'd taken covertly using a camera hidden in my bathroom.

"That was five years ago and technology still scares me. I often leave my phone at home because I have a fear of being watched and tracked."

Using the Children to Abuse

"He used the children to trap me – it worked."

Using children as weapons

Abusive fathers use children as weapons to control their intimate partners. These men seemingly have little regard for the damage caused to their children: domestic abuse has a devastating impact on them. Children of every social class and culture are affected by witnessing domestic abuse in the home. It causes children distress, anxiety, it negatively affects their learning, educational achievement, wellbeing and life chances. (Sterne, 2009[28])

Children witnessing domestic abuse are being emotionally abused and this is classed as 'significant harm' in UK law. Abusive fathers use their children in a variety of different ways to perpetuate domestic abuse. Using children is highly effective as a way of exerting power and control over their intimate partners or former partners.

- Men with jealous and possessive tendencies may know their partner is more likely to stay in the relationship if they have a child together. A child makes leaving more difficult. Abusive men may push for an early pregnancy as a means of reducing their partner's ability to leave the relationship.
- Abusive men may also keep women pregnant as a means of controlling them. When pregnant, women are more vulnerable, both physically and emotionally, and abusive men are more likely to assault their partner when she is pregnant. Domestic abuse during pregnancy has serious consequences, increasing the risk of miscarriage, infection, premature birth, injury or death of the baby.

Stress and anxiety can also be passed to the developing baby. Pregnant women are not likely to have their needs met when living with domestic abuse. Ideally, they should have a calm environment, good nutrition, and practical and emotional support from a partner who will prioritise their needs. This is not likely when their partner is abusive and when they live in fear of physical and emotional assault. (Martin & Hunt, 2000[29])

- Women and children are abused when the father manipulates and controls the mother's contact with children. He may abuse her by refusing to allow her to attend to her crying baby. He may demand that she bottle-feeds and shouldn't share her body with the baby. He may not allow her to show affection to young children if he is around. Being unable to respond properly to her children's needs is damaging to both mother and her child and can make it more difficult for her to bond with her child.

Keeping women at home

We know that many abusive men like to keep women at home, away from work and isolated from others. Abusive fathers may control by neglecting their parental responsibilities, so women are restricted in their ability to go out or return to work. He may agree to care for the children but do it so badly by leaving them screaming in soiled nappies and unfed, that she won't dare leave them with him again. He may 'allow' her out, then phone her every time the baby cries, holding the phone to the baby so that her time out with friends is wrecked. Children prove very useful in keeping women imprisoned in the home. Women may not flee the abuse because they would feel guilty for breaking up the family and depriving the children of a father. Abusive fathers often blame the mother for breaking up the family. Other family members may blame the mother too, and so the easiest option is often to stay.

Inability to leave the abusive relationship

The most common reason for children being taken into care is because the mother has not left an abusive relationship despite numerous demands by social care to do so. The damage this action causes is immense. These women become broken and they are often shunned by family and friends for 'choosing' to stay in the relationship. Often, they don't have a free choice to leave because their partner won't allow it. The resulting trauma can be catastrophic to both mothers and their children, who are being raised in the care system.

Knowing how angry her partner can be or how neglectful he is in terms of childcare, a woman may not want to leave because after separation the abusive father would be unsupervised during contact. The thought of the children being unprotected from his rages might be enough for her to not dare to leave.

Abusing alcohol and drugs

Women's ability to respond appropriately to their children's needs may be compromised by the impact of domestic abuse. It's not uncommon for survivors to abuse alcohol and controlled or prescription drugs.

Anxiety and depression are also common features in survivors. Sometimes, but not always, women in these situations may be less responsive to their children's needs, and as a result might become less effective and less competent mothers. Abusive fathers may use this situation against them when it suits – by threatening to report the mother to social care if she threatens to leave or by using social media to tell family and friends she's a neglectful mother. The stigma and trauma that mothers then feel is intense.

Mistreatment of children

If women do separate, men may emotionally burden the children during contact, which in turn emotionally burdens the mother. He may tell them he's sad and lonely and missing them. He may say he has no money to buy food and might starve. He may say he loves Mummy and feels so sad she doesn't love him anymore. The children will feel terrible and may try to persuade their mother to renew the relationship. She will feel emotionally burdened by this and will be acutely aware of the damage this causes to the children.

- Separated, abusive fathers may feed children junk food, fail to impose bedtimes, allow continual screen use and inappropriate movies, sometimes pornography. These men may overindulge children with presents and fail to impose boundaries. They may undermine the mother by doing this and she will find imposing rules and discipline challenging after the children's time with him. His behaviour will often be designed to undermine her. He may go further and more actively undermine her parenting by telling the children she's boring, that they should disobey her and that they should tell her they want to live with him. Children often become conflicted, confused, badly behaved and emotionally damaged. Mothers can find themselves unable to impose discipline and unable to protect their children from this toxic emotional abuse.

- Abusive fathers sometimes encourage misogyny (dislike of women and prejudice against them) in their sons. They will role-model abuse of women and actively encourage their sons to disregard female authority. This behaviour is damaging to the mother and children involved and perpetuates domestic abuse by encouraging gender stereotypes based on the notion of male superiority.
- Because they're bullies, abusive fathers will commonly behave in a bullying and undermining manner towards their children. These fathers will sometimes berate their sons for crying and demonstrating 'weakness'. Yelling *"man up, don't be a pussy"* to a crying 6-year-old boy and showing insensitivity towards children's emotions is directly emotionally abusive. With daughters, they may display similar intolerance and bullying behaviours. They may trivialise daughters, praise them only for their appearance, call them stupid and expect them to help their mothers with menial tasks. This abuse of children will clearly impact the mother emotionally, too.

Child contact arrangements

Following separation, women are often abused through child contact arrangements. Fathers who have previously shown little or no interest in the children sometimes actively pursue contact as a means of continuing to abuse the mother. He may turn up on her doorstep unannounced, demanding to see the children but using this as an excuse to abuse, harass and terrorise. Men will also use child contact as an excuse to have contact with the mother because they are jealous, possessive and unwilling to give up the relationship. These men may use child contact as an excuse to be sexually inappropriate and even to rape their former partner. Children provide a link that allows abusive men long-term access to survivors who find themselves unable to escape from the abuse.

- Men may apply to the courts for Child Arrangements Orders with the sole intention of abusing the mother further. Abusive fathers may seek access to their children to gain power and control over the mother. The Family Courts will regularly disregard domestic abuse as a reason to suggest a father should not have contact or should have limited contact with his children. Mothers who voice concerns about the father often will be accused by the courts of parental alienation – wilfully turning the children against their father.
- Many of the professionals involved in the court process, including judges, lack appropriate training about domestic abuse. They will routinely dismiss rape and domestic abuse as either false or irrelevant to a child's welfare. These people may not be aware that the charming father expressing concerns about his estranged wife's mental health is exhibiting classic perpetrator behaviour. Children are often scared and traumatised by their father, however, until they are around 10 years old, their wishes are given little acknowledgement by the courts. Many women experience the horror

of being ordered to hand over terrorised children to their abusive fathers and being unable to do anything to protect the children.

- Even when agreements or court orders are in place around child contact, abusive men may abuse women and cause emotional damage to children by unreliable and intermittent contact. These men may disrupt the survivor's holiday plans or ensure that she can never count on him to be reliable enough to allow her to plan her work commitments around his contact with them. She will feel awful when she must deal with the emotional fallout when he doesn't collect the children as promised. He might move on to a new partner and have more children who he favours and prioritises, causing serious feelings of rejection in his older children.

Financial abuse

Financial abuse involving fathers refusing to pay maintenance for their children is common. If he does pay, he may decide to pay what's owed directly into the child's account in an act that reduces the mother's ability to spend this money appropriately. Some abusive fathers refuse to allow the children to take anything bought by him to their mother's house. He may also 'lose' essential items such as school shoes when the children are in his care, forcing the mother to buy another pair. Some men will fail to provide adequate food to the point that mothers will feel compelled to send food when they go to their father for the weekend, to avoid them coming home starving.

The ultimate abuse

On rare occasions, men will murder their children as an ultimate act of abuse. On 1st April 2020 in West Sussex, Robert Needham shot dead his partner Kelly Fitzgibbons and two young children before turning the gun on himself. For every tragic murder involving children, countless more women will fear this act of revenge. Just the threat or fear that their children might not be safe will encourage women to stay with the perpetrator and do as he demands. Threats to kill are commonly made by abusive men but there is often little the police can do to prosecute. To charge men with making such threats, first there needs to be proof that the threat was made and secondly that he intended the threat to be believed, this can prove difficult.

Using children as a way of abusing their mothers

In many ways, the use of children to abuse their mothers is the most insidious form of abuse, but as with other forms of abuse, women are often highly conflicted. She will commonly claim he is a good father despite the fact he actively abuses her and undermines her mothering. She will say he loves the children even when he emotionally abuses them. She will remain in an abusive relationship 'for the sake of the children' or if she moves on, she may blame herself for 'breaking up the family'. She will 'try to be fair' around child contact even when met with a total lack of fairness from him. Professional support is often needed to help women and their children when they are exposed to this devastating abuse.

- The outcomes for children exposed to domestic abuse can be worrying. Each child responds differently to trauma, some have high levels of resilience, others suffer more. Exposure can cause children to suffer symptoms including anxiety, depression, self-harm, aggressive outbursts, withdrawn behaviour, low self-worth, and problems with alcohol and drugs in later life.
- The use of children to abuse their mother is terrible for all exposed to it. Mothers are right to be highly concerned and sometimes the damage caused is profound. This said, mothers can do much to mitigate the potential damage caused by this abuse. If children have one good, caring, responsive, supportive and loving parent, this is often enough to nurture and guide the child towards a healthy and happy adult life.

How do abusive fathers affect women?

- Women often feel unable to leave an abusive relationship when they share children with their abuser.
- If women do leave, it can be impossible for them to protect themselves from continuing abuse when they are forced to communicate about child contact.
- When they have no-one to act as a third party for handing over the children, women may need to have face-to-face contact with their

abuser. This situation can make them vulnerable to further emotional, physical and sexual abuse.

- When still in contact with their abuser, it may be more difficult for women to recover from their trauma.
- Women may suffer significant trauma when they have concerns about the safety of children in their father's care. There is often little that women can do to protect the children from their father's abuse and this can be torturous for them.
- When children have been traumatised by their father's behaviour, women may have significant challenges trying to parent their children. They can be left feeling exhausted and desperate.

Tips for surviving the abusive father

How to survive the abusive father and protect the children, too, is a very difficult subject. In general terms, open your eyes to the abuse your children are being subjected to – the damage it can cause is immense and keeping the family together is not likely to be the best solution. Also, you might be less effective as a mother when undermined by abuse. Women often stay in abusive relationships for too long because they don't want to break up the family, but it is damaging to children to witness abuse, so leaving might be the most protective thing you can do for your children.

If you separate, limit your contact with your abuser post-separation if this is possible. If he continues to be abusive, do what you can to reduce his ability to communicate with you – for instance, keep communication to email only and just discuss child-related matters. Consider even more indirect means of communication, for instance a book that is passed between you and the father during child contact and you both agree to write in it only about child related matters. There are apps such as the 'amicable co-parenting app' that might help you to communicate child contact issues more easily. If you're abused while handing the children over, try to get a third party to do this for you, or ask a friend to accompany you while this is done.

You may imagine that the Family Court will help protect you and your children and that a Child Arrangements Order might make negotiating contact easier when there has been abuse. Sadly, as mentioned earlier, the Family Courts are highly motivated to encourage a relationship between children and fathers, and there is rarely a good outcome for women who hope the courts will positively intervene when domestic abuse occurs. That said, if the abuse is serious, the Family Courts may impose some safeguarding measures to help keep children protected from their abusive fathers, so you must consider the courts to be an option, particularly with serious abuse.

If you worry that they're being emotionally abused, you may consider reporting your concerns about your children to their school or to the police, or making a child safeguarding referral to the local authority. You should document all instances of child abuse and abuse that took place in front of your children. Whether logged onto a Word document or in a diary, notes made at the time will add credibility to any accounts given to others.

If possible, seeking support from your wider family and friends can be helpful. If children are estranged from abusive fathers, other family members can be of huge help in providing practical and emotional support.

Remember that separating from an abusive partner can be dangerous and needs to be carefully considered and well-planned. Separation also becomes more difficult when children are involved as you're not likely to be able to sever all ties with your abuser. Feeling guilt about separating the children from their father is normal – most women do. However, you're likely to be doing the best thing for them and yourself by leaving the relationship. If you're feeling guilty for not leaving earlier and you blame yourself for the damage caused to the children – again it is normal to feel like this, but remind yourself, he caused the damage, not you. You can only leave when you feel you are able to.

Beth's Story

"When I look back, I was always in denial about Jack's abuse of our children. I knew he was a vile and controlling husband, but I maintained he was a good father despite his frequent rages that would leave the children in tears. I felt hideously guilty for leaving him. I believed the children would suffer when the family split up, that I was putting my needs first, but I was no longer able to tolerate his abuse. It wasn't until we left that he stepped up his campaign against me and deliberately used the children to punish me. His emotional manipulation was terrible, he would cry in front of them and tell them his life was worthless without us. He told them he couldn't afford to eat properly because I'd taken all the money, that he was lonely and sad and had nothing to look forward to. We had a wobbly

year with the children feeling sad, confused and conflicted following weekends with him. But everything changed when he met Steph, his current partner. Jack and Steph are expecting a baby and he no longer wants to see our children. He started making excuses that he was busy when he was due to have them. He'd be late to collect them and early to drop them back and now it's been six months since he had any contact. They've struggled with this rejection, but they are no longer being exposed to his emotional abuse. I do my best to reassure them. I try to make up for his rejection of them, but this is difficult, they feel it badly. On the plus side, both sets of grandparents are amazing and actively involved in the children's lives. This has helped enormously. I'm not sure how we'd have coped without their support."

Trauma Bonding

"I know he can be mean but I love him so much."

"For me, the abuse was what felt like a constant stream of toxicity. It was a never-ending barrage of being told I was worthless, being emotionally and physically abused, and feeling undeserving of my existence. Through this horrible toxic fog, I would sometimes get glimmers of the man I met. The funny one, the loving one, the one who made me happy. Though these instances were few and far between, and I craved them so much, they were actually part of a calculated plan on his part."
– Kozlowski, 2020[20]

What are trauma bonds?

Survivors and perpetrators of domestic abuse will often form trauma bonds which causes them both to become emotionally hooked into the relationship – this can make it extremely difficult for the survivor to unlock herself and escape from the abuse. The survivor will feel a very strong connection with her abusive partner. The intensity of love felt by the survivor towards her abuser often appears stronger than in healthy relationships. She will feel sympathy for him and intense loyalty towards him, not despite his abuse but rather because of his abuse.

"Trauma, fear and abandonment actually increase feelings of attachment. The more you have been hurt by him, the more intensely attached you will be. Trauma bonds are hard to break but even harder to live with."
– Hill, 2020[30]

How do trauma bonds develop?

Trauma bonding doesn't just happen – it takes time to develop this toxic and harmful bond. They aren't inevitable either, many women will not become trauma bonded. The abuser will deliberately weaken his partner and create a power imbalance before he is able to hold this sort of control over her. Typical narcissistic behaviour will make women vulnerable to developing trauma bonds. Very often abuse will start with 'love bombing' – where the abuser will overwhelm his new partner with loving behaviour as a means of manipulating her. Isolation often follows – he will do what he can to reduce her contact with others as a means of increasing her dependency on him and may try to force her out of work, too. Without the support of family, friends and colleagues, she will begin to depend on her abuser for validation and he will give her validation initially. Once she becomes reliant upon him, he will start criticising her. This might be subtle, where he hopes she won't realise what he's doing, or it may be more overt. He might start to 'gaslight' her – make her question her own reality so she loses confidence in her judgment and may depend more on him. This behaviour will cause a loss of self-worth in the woman and she will feel increasingly reliant on her abuser. The abuser will gain control and she will try desperately to please him and to win validation from him. The trauma bond will develop. Her abuser has destroyed her confidence, but she will feel he is the only person who can make her feel worthy again. She will desperately seek his validation and he will cruelly manipulate her need most of the time. Occasionally, he will reward her with kindness. On the rare occasions when he is kind, she will doubt he was ever properly abusive and blame herself for not trying harder in the relationship.

By providing intermittent rewards and punishments (occasional kind and loving gestures, together with cruel, hostile behaviour) at irregular intervals, a psychological conditioning develops. Like a slot machine offering intermittent payouts, the survivor becomes ensnared in the relationship, ever hopeful of the next reward and a reprieve from the abuse and suffering.

When we are traumatised and our safety is threatened, we turn to someone who can offer support, protection and care. This person is often our intimate partner, even when he has caused the trauma. This is particularly likely when we're isolated from others due to his abuse. We feel attachment towards our partner when he provides comfort. This attachment strengthens the trauma bonds which are extremely resistant to change. (Kozlowski, 2020[20])

How are trauma bonds sustained?

Once the trauma bond has been established, it is reinforced further with cycles of abuse. Following an abusive incident or series of incidents, abusive men will often offer some affection, enough to remind his partner how loving he can be. A period of relative calm can follow before tensions start to rebuild and the abuse inevitably starts again. Women will try their best not to anger their partner. If he is angry, she will blame herself, and will do everything expected of her, remembering how loving her partner can be and hoping for the return of that behaviour. She will think she just needs to work out what she's doing wrong to bring back the good part of their relationship. She'll become obsessed with winning his affection. It won't occur to her that his kind gestures were manipulative and not genuine, her partner being incapable of real and sustained love. The longer the survivor remains with the narcissistic abuser, the more difficult it becomes to break the trauma bond.

Cognitive dissonance

When the abuser alternates between nice and nasty, the survivor will be confused as to which is the real person. Is he kind, loving and generous, or is he hostile, abusive and angry? These conflicting thoughts create cognitive dissonance – mental confusion from holding two conflicting beliefs. The cognitive dissonance experienced undermines the survivor and helps strengthen the trauma bond.

> *"He broke my nose, then the neighbours heard my screams and called the police. I pleaded with them that I'd fallen over but they didn't believe me and arrested him. I was distraught. I'd have said anything to get him released."*
> *– Survivor*

The abuser will try to win you back

If women manage to break free from the trauma bond, the abuser will commonly revert to the courtship phase in an attempt to win his partner back. Women may be extremely vulnerable to the abuser's efforts. Abusive men are experts at manipulative persuasion. He will struggle to deal with the loss of control that comes with his partner leaving him. This is a very dangerous time because he will do everything in his power to persuade his partner back into the relationship. Very often, his persuasive tactics pay off and she returns to the relationship. Following the initial 'honeymoon' period, the abuse will inevitably begin again, the trauma bond will be strengthened and the destructive cycle continues.

> *"Periods of kindness, however short, bond the victim to her abuser."*
> *– Hill, 2020*

How trauma bonding affects women

- Trauma-bonded women have massive difficulty leaving their abuser. Their attachment is likely to be stronger than in a non-abusive relationship. They may also lack confidence due to the abuse, which will make the task of leaving feel even more difficult.
- Women who are trauma bonded may leave on several occasions, only to return to the abusive relationship when they find the intensity of desire for their abuser too strong to resist.
- Abusive men will understand what women in trauma bonds most crave and they will manipulate and play on their partner's weaknesses to stay in control of the relationship. This makes women

very vulnerable to further abuse and hyper-focused on pleasing the perpetrator.

- Women who experience trauma bonding may not feel as devoted and committed to a healthy, subsequent relationship because they don't feel the same intensity of attachment. On occasions they may return to their abusive, former partner.
- Women who have been in trauma bonds often suffer deep psychological trauma long after the relationship has ended. They will often say they're still in love with their abuser even when they understand how abusive he was.
- Trauma bonding will often lead to depression and anxiety.
- Women in this situation are sometimes continually tortured by being forced to have ongoing contact with their abuser.
- Women who are trauma bonded will feel intense pain when they see their partner in a new intimate relationship.

Tips for surviving a trauma bond

- If still with the abuser, admit the reality of your relationship, stop minimising the abuse and understand it will only get worse. Pay attention to the cycles of abuse.
- Physically separate from the abuser if possible. Although this can be difficult, it's invariably easier than emotional separation. If you can, move away so you are never likely to bump into him again.
- Cut off all lines of communication as far as possible. This can be made almost impossible if you share children. However, restricting

communication to just email for instance, or through a third party for childcare-related matters, might be possible.

- Understand that you deserve better. Ask yourself if you'd be happy if your daughter was treated like this. Would your friends accept this sort of treatment?
- Acknowledge that you have a choice and can choose to leave the relationship. When choice is acknowledged, it is possible to gain control and drive your destiny with less vulnerability to further abuse.
- Self-reflection will enable you to understand how your character traits played a part in a co-dependent bond. Being abused is never your fault. However, there may be aspects of your personality that made you more susceptible to becoming trauma bonded (for example, high levels of empathy).
- Work out what hooked you into this abusive relationship: was it a fantasy or an illusion of a perfect future? Did your partner convince you that he would meet some deepfelt need in you? Were you hoping he would make up for something you felt you were lacking?
- Learn about the character traits of narcissistic abusers because this will help you understand what happened to you so that you will be less susceptible to future abusive relationships.
- Develop a support network of professionals, and trusted friends and family members who will actively, positively and compassionately support you to recover from the trauma bond. Domestic abuse is an isolating experience but prioritising social connections is vital for recovery.

- Make decisions that support your self-care. Be self-compassionate and don't berate yourself for 'mistakes'; see recovery as a work in progress and life as a journey.
- Learn to self-validate and establish your own worthiness so you don't need to look externally for validation.
- Live in the present and notice how you're feeling now. If you're still in the relationship, notice how trapped you feel, notice how scared and unloved you feel. Notice how you have compromised your self-worth for this relationship. Stop hoping for things to be better in the future but notice how you're feeling now.
- Accept sadness and realise you must grieve the end of an intense and abusive relationship. Don't expect to feel better too soon but have confidence that better times will come.
- Write a list of what you would refuse to tolerate in a future relationship (for example, *'I will not be intimate with someone who calls me names', 'I refuse to be questioned every time I go out', 'I will wear what I like', 'I will not have conversations with someone when I feel desperate or obsessive.')*
- If you find your mind flitting between the good times and the bad times and trying to make sense of what was real, writing a timeline of your relationship noting the good and bad times can help. You are likely to see that the good times are bunched up near the beginning of the relationship and the bad times start appearing after that. You will see that the good times become fewer and you may consider how this would be likely to get worse if the relationship was continued.

Miranda's Story

"I've never felt more in love with someone, nor more broken at the same time. My feelings for Oliver were intense, I was completely addicted. I was obsessed with trying to make him proud of me. I'd lost everything so all my focus was on him. I needed him and wanted him so badly. I had no family or friends left to turn to. Oliver was partly to blame for that, he made things difficult and then they blamed me for continuing with what they told me was an abusive relationship. I didn't see it like that, I do now.

"I don't think I'd have had the strength to end the relationship if Oliver hadn't been locked up. He was convicted of causing death by dangerous driving and given a four-year sentence. It wasn't so much what he'd done that appalled me, although that was bad enough. It was more his reaction. He felt no remorse, none at all. All he could think of was himself. He'd always just thought about himself though, the classic narcissist. I forced myself not to visit him in prison, this was torture, but I knew it was my best chance to break the bond. I went through a form of bereavement, I felt I still loved him, but I knew that was no longer enough. I read and reflected and started to understand what had happened to me. It's been hard but I know I'm in a better place now. I've worked to rebuild my confidence. I'm determined never to be abused like that again."

New Relationship Checklist

"He made me feel so special, I now realise he was too good to be true."

We can learn to protect ourselves from the abusive manipulator. We can read the warning signs and choose to walk away.

Domestic abuse has a devastating impact on survivors and its effects are often felt long after the relationship has ended. With one in four women suffering domestic abuse at some point in their lives, and many being repeat survivors, it is important to do everything possible to avoid further abuse. Women who have suffered abuse will often not want to risk another relationship for fear of being abused again. But we can educate ourselves so we become less vulnerable to an abuser's advances. We can also prepare our daughters so they are more able to protect themselves.

Abusive men span all social classes, age groups and ethnic backgrounds. However, they commonly display several patterns of behaviour from very early in a relationship. If we are aware of these traits, tread cautiously, listen to our intuition and are prepared to back out fast, we can help protect ourselves from becoming prey to an abuser.

Character traits to be wary of in a prospective partner or new partner

- **Jealousy** is a very common trait of abusive men which is often displayed early on, so be on the alert for the very first signs. At the start of a relationship, the abuser will equate jealousy with love. When women are not familiar with displays of jealousy, this behaviour can seem very appealing and attractive to them. Jealousy can make us feel special, that he wants us so badly and wants to spend all his time with us to the exclusion of everyone else. Jealousy can be very seductive and can make us vulnerable to falling quickly into the predator's trap. The abuser may accuse us of flirting, he may monitor who we speak to, phone us frequently during the day and drop by our workplace unexpectedly. He may also check our car mileage, control what we wear and ask friends to watch us. Behaviour like this, that might initially appear as deep love, will often escalate to more serious and overt abuse that can include locking the survivor in the house or electronically tracking her movements.

- **The charming manipulator.** In 2017, Sandra Horley wrote 'Power and Control: why charming men can make dangerous lovers'[9] which explains that many abusive men are highly charming and suggests that charm is a risk factor for domestic abuse. Narcissistic manipulators are often charismatic and charming, particularly at the start of a relationship and also around others. Of course, not all charming men are abusive. However, women should be aware of this trait and its links with abuse.

- **Showing off around others.** Narcissistic men 'feed off' others, not just their intimate partners. They often like to be the centre of attention, to be looked up to and admired by others. These men may thrive when showing off to an audience. This will be a front to mask insecurities, but may not appear so until you know him better. Be wary of the showman!

- **Passive aggression.** Covert narcissists may sulk, withdraw eye contact and behave in a passive aggressive manner. They use more subtle methods to signal their dissatisfaction. It may be difficult for women to pinpoint what is wrong, but she will feel her partner's tension and angry mood even when he doesn't say anything.

- **Controlling behaviour** is closely related to jealousy. Like jealousy, this behaviour can also appeal to women in the early stages, especially when jealousy is often dressed up as concern for her welfare. The perpetrator may insist on accompanying the survivor everywhere, explaining he wants to keep her safe. He may take control of her finances, stating that he wants to spare her the trouble. He may choose her clothes, telling her he knows what suits her best. As this behaviour inevitably progresses, the situation generally worsens, often to the point where women's lives become massively restricted and they are able to make very few choices.

- **Fast-tracked love – 'love bombing'.** Perpetrators of abuse will commonly fast-track the early stages of a relationship. They want to encourage women to fall for them as quickly as possible because a woman in love is more vulnerable. Men may do this with gushing gestures of adoration and expressions of love. They do everything possible to seem indispensable to their partner and encourage her to believe that they were meant to be together. Again, this behaviour is highly flattering, it makes women feel special, and this means they are likely to reciprocate the love and adoration. Fast-tracked love is often fake, the gestures insincere. Once in love, women will be more likely put up with abusive behaviour. She'll also feel very confused and however bad the abuse gets, she'll keep remembering the early days when he showered her with adoration. She may hold on to the relationship, believing that things will get better. They rarely do.

- **Isolation** is a tactic used by abusive men. Again, this behaviour can be flattering initially. He purports to be so in love with her that he wants her all to himself. He may suggest a whole weekend in bed and cancel arrangements with family and friends because he wants only to be with her. As time progresses, the isolation tactics become more overtly abusive and can progress to threatening her about making social contacts or becoming openly hostile to her family when they visit.

- **Unhappy childhood.** Disclosures of bad childhoods and difficult pasts will elicit sympathy in women who may be motivated to try harder to make the relationship work and be more understanding and tolerant of poor behaviour. Abusive men often have troubled childhoods, which may be part of the reason they became abusers. Women need to remember that it's not their fault he was abused as a child, and it's not likely she can do anything to repair that damage. When abusers go too far, they'll often remind women about their terrible pasts and 'guilt-trip' women for being just another person who gives up on them. Abusers are good at emotional blackmail. Women in this situation are often conflicted and confused enough to continue with the relationship despite the abuse.

- **Blaming others for their feelings and problems.** Abusive men often blame others and most often the survivor for their own mistakes, problems and how they feel. Abusers are skilled at coercion and manipulation. In the early stages, he may tell the survivor that he's upset because she's not spending enough time with him, or that she's going out with her girlfriends when she knows how much he's been missing her. These comments make women feel that his distress is her fault. This manipulative blame may escalate as the relationship progresses. *"You were flirting so you made me hit you." "You wouldn't have sex, so I had to find someone else." "It's your fault I threw the dinner at the wall, it was disgusting."* It's very easy for the survivor to believe it really is her fault as this will make sense in the early stages. The alternative would be to acknowledge that the man she's fallen in love with is a monster and she'd generally rather not do that. Instead, she'll tell herself she just needs to try harder and give him more attention and love and things will be fine again.

- **Hypersensitivity to personal attack.** Abusive men are easily insulted and offended, perceiving the slightest thing as a personal attack. Women may tell themselves to be more sensitive and show more consideration towards his feelings. His sensitivity might seem appealing initially. His sensitivity will be less appealing when he is holding a fist in her face and yelling at her for telling him the picture he's just hung is crooked. Linked with this is an inability to apologise. Women often find themselves apologising for his mistakes, anticipating they will be blamed anyway. Of course, abusive men will sometimes apologise to try to recover the situation when they recognise that they have gone too far with their abuse. When he's seemingly unable to apologise for the little things, this should be seen as a 'red flag' in any relationship.

- **The evil ex-girlfriend.** Abusive men will likely leave a trail of abused former girlfriends behind them. They're not likely to admit to being abusive and will generally lie about their previous girlfriends, often accusing them of the behaviour of which they themselves are guilty of. Be very wary of a man who has a Restraining Order or Non-Molestation Order relating to a former partner. Expect them to lie outrageously about the circumstances of how this came about. Be aware of any evidence of a police caution or criminal conviction for assault.

What you can do if you have concerns about a new partner

Claire's Law (also known as the Domestic Violence Disclosure Scheme). If you have serious concerns about your safety with your partner or former partner, you, or someone representing you, could approach the police and ask for a disclosure under Claire's Law. The police may be able to disclose details of your partner's previous abusive or violent offending. The police can disclose intelligence they hold, as well as details of cautions and criminal convictions, if relevant. This information may help you decide how to proceed. Remember that there will be a lot of abusive men for whom the police hold no information at all, so if the police have nothing to disclose, your concerns and worries are still likely to be valid.

What do your friends think? Good friends can be more objective than you because they're not invested in the relationship. Friends might feel uncomfortable about your new partner. They may take the risk of telling you what they've noticed, but often they don't and will keep their concerns private. If you have good and trustworthy friends, it can be worth asking them what they think of your new partner. If they express concerns, listen to them and consider acting on their concerns.

Gut instinct counts. Because domestic abuse is often intended to confuse, we may feel terrible in a relationship but not understand why. The abuse could be very subtle, often repeated micro-aggressions, with frequent blame, so we may imagine things are our fault. Even if we can't consciously work out what is happening, our sub-conscious is more perceptive and will tell us when things are wrong. If our gut instinct and intuition give us warning signals, it's best to act on this and distance ourselves from the relationship. Many women who have been abused by narcissistic men admit that they felt things weren't right, that the warnings signs were there and their gut instinct had warned them, but they chose to ignore these feelings and lived to regret it.

What is worrying is that, paradoxically, early warning traits are often so appealing to women. For this reason, it's as well to be aware of these traits and actively look out for them to avoid being seduced by them and drawn in. The earlier women can walk away from an abusive relationship, the easier this will be and the less damage will be caused. The start of a potential relationship is a time when women need to have their wits about them. At this time, it really is essential to use your head, your intuition, listen to the opinions of friends and family, and be prepared to bail out fast.

Samantha's Story

"I'd heard terrible things about Sean before we got together and never imagined I'd have been interested in a relationship with someone like him, but he seemed lovely, kind, warm and funny. Not at all the person I'd been warned about. I decided to take him as I found him rather than listening to gossip. He told me about his ex-girlfriend at the start, he knew that I would have heard rumours. His version was that she couldn't cope when he decided to end things, so she injured herself and complained to the police that he'd assaulted her. This made sense to me because I believed that some women can be lying manipulators. He said that because she had an injury, they believed her and he was convicted of ABH.

"My friends continued to warn me off Sean, but I wouldn't listen – until I saw a few flashes of his anger. He never hit me but on a couple of occasions I saw his rage for the first time and I worried about what he might be capable of. Doubt crept in, so when one of my friends suggested that I ask for a 'Claire's Law' disclosure, I decided to do it. What I found out was beyond shocking and I now feel I had a lucky escape. The police also advised me how to end the relationship safely. I was lucky because I was able to work remotely, so I stayed at my parent's address in Liverpool until I decided it was safe to come back, which happened pretty soon because Sean breached his licence and was back in prison. He'd been convicted of inflicting GBH on his former girlfriend. He broke her jaw and several ribs; he'd served three years of a six-year

sentence and had been released on licence only a month before we met. He had a long history of assault convictions including other domestic assaults. I would have become his next victim; it was just a matter of time."

More Information

Please visit my website – **www.domesticabuses.com** for:

- Survivors' stories
- Domestic abuse blogs
- Coaching for recovery
- Links to legal information
- Wellbeing pages
- The Survivors' Programme
- Current developments in domestic abuse

Please Review

Thank you for buying and reading this book.

I want to reach as many readers as possible so if you've found it helpful, I'd be very grateful if you would take the time to write a review on Amazon.

Thank you!

References

[1] Hill, Jess (2020), See What You Made Me Do: Power, Control and Domestic Abuse, C. Hurst & Co Publishers Ltd: London

[2] Freeland, Cynthia, (1998), Feminist Interpretations of Aristotle, Pennsylvania University Press: Philadelphia

[3] (2018), End Violence Towards Women – Attitudes to Sexual Consent, You Gov: London

[4] Bates, Laura (2019), Misogynation, Simon & Schuster: London

[5] Gracie, Carrie (2019), Equal – A Story of Women, Men and Money, Little Brown Book Group: London

[6] Eminem (2000), Kill You, Producers: Dr Dre, Eminem, F.B.T., Mel Man, The 45 King (This is a recording of a song)

[7] Cikanavicius, Darius (2018), Human Development and Trauma: How Childhood Shapes Us Into Who We Are As Adults, Independently published

[8] Stark, Evan (2007), Coercive Control: How Men Entrap Women in Personal Life, Oxford University Press: Oxford

[9] Horley, Sandra (2017) Power and Control: Why Charming Men Can Make Dangerous Lovers, Ebury Publishing: London

[10] Monckton Smith, Jane (2021), In Control – Dangerous Relationships and How They End, Bloomsbury Publishing: London

[11] Maslow, Abraham (1954), Motivation and Personality, Harper & Brothers: New York

[12] Brownmiller, Susan (1975), Against Our Will: Men, Women and Rape, Secker and Warburg: London

[13] Penny, Laurie (2015), Unspeakable Things. Sex, Lies and Revolution, Bloomsbury: London

[14] Brodsky, Alexandra (2017), Rape – Adjacent: Imagining Legal Responses to Non-consensual Condom Removal, Columbia Journal of Gender and Law Vol. 32, No. 2: New York

[15] James, E L (2012), Fifty Shades of Grey, Arrow: London

[16] Thompson, Rachel (2021), Rough: How violence has found its way into the bedroom, Penguin, Random House: London

[17] Lowen, Alexander (1997), Narcissism, Touchstone: New York

[18] Thomas, Shannon (2016), Healing from Hidden Abuse: A Journey Through the Stages of Recovery from Psychological Abuse, MAST Publishing: Arizona

[19] Sarkis, Stephanie (2019), Gaslighting: How to Recognise Manipulative and Emotionally Abusive People - and Break Free, Orion Publishing Group Ltd: London

[20] Kozlowski, Lauren (2020), Trauma Bonding: Understanding and Overcoming the Trauma Bond in a Narcissistic Relationship, Lauren Kozlowski Publications

[21] Taylor, Jessica Dr (2021), Why Women are Blamed for Everything, Constable: UK

[22] Snyder, Rachel Louise (2020), No Visible Bruises – what we don't know about domestic violence can kill us, Scribe Publications: London

[23] Goldman, Emma (1970), Anarchism and Other Essays, Dover Publications Inc: New York

[24] Joshi, Heather & Paci, Pierella (1998), Unequal Pay for Women and Men: Evidence from The British Birth Cohort Studies, MIT Press: Massachusetts

[25] Dowling et al (2014), Problem Gambling and Intimate Partner Violence: A Systematic Review and Meta-Analysis, Sage Publications: Washington

[26] Thomas, Shannon (2018), Exposing Financial Abuse, When Money is a Weapon, MAST Publishing: Arizona

[27] Sting (1983), Every Breath You Take, Song by the band 'The Police' from the album Synchronicity, Producer: Hugh Padgham

[28] Sterne, Abigail & Poole, Liz (2009), Domestic Violence and Children – a handbook for schools and early years settings, Routledge: Oxfordshire

[29] Martin, Ann & Hunt, Sheila (2000), Pregnant Women, Violent Men: What Midwives Need to Know, Elsevier: Amsterdam

[30] Hill, Jess (2020), See What You Made Me Do: Power, Control and Domestic Abuse, C. Hurst & Co Publishers Ltd: London

Printed in Great Britain
by Amazon

11498445R00098